URBAN GREEN

CITY PARKS OF THE WESTERN WORLD
URBAN GREEN

JERE STUART FRENCH

California State Polytechnic University - Pomona

KENDALL/HUNT PUBLISHING COMPANY
DUBUQUE, IOWA

FOR JOAN

CREDITS

Photography:

Los Angeles Recreation and Parks Department
Chicago Park District
Aerospace Corporation, Los Angeles
Amsterdam Department of Parks
Illustrated London News
Ateljé Sundahl AB, Stockholm
Parkavdelningen, Stockholm
Peter Blöm, Stockholm
Gösta Glase, Stockholm
Reposbagebeld, Stockholm
Eric Rosenberg, Stockholm
Text and Bilder, Stockholm
Dienst Publicke Werken, Amsterdam
Leif Persson, Stockholm
Greater London Council
Louis Robinson
Harvey Steinberg
The Author

Drawings:

Tita Thomas
Michael Williams
Chan Chan Kwong
James Gilray
Students, School of Environmental Design,
    California State Polytechnic University
The Author

Also special thanks to Bernard Zavidowsky and Joan French
for their most valuable assistance in preparation of the text.

CONTENTS

PROLOGUE

One hot, smoggy evening in late summer, the elected council of a small Los Angeles suburb had gathered in special session to discuss the possibility of obtaining a seven-acre park site. The parcel of land, the last of a once productive lemon grove, was to be a gift to the city from a civic minded, tax weary grower.

As their consultant, I urged the members of the council to act quickly, since this acquisition would more than double the city's park acreage (for a population of over 6000!), and provide badly needed open space to that section of the city which had in recent years become overcrowded with small tract houses.

The air conditioning had been turned off in the council chambers at five o'clock by the departing office staff. A councilman wiped his brow and squinted through the window at the sinking sun, bloated and discolored by the polluted atmosphere of eastern Los Angeles County. "Why should we add further burden to our taxpayers when no one uses the park we have?"

True enough. Once an open square of green bordered by small shops and a cluster of civic buildings, the old park had shaped the town's center with grace and dignity; moreover, it had provided a center in the true meaning of the word—a gathering place, an urban nucleus where shoppers and shopkeepers, residents, kids, retired folk and passersby might come together—even briefly—in the time honored exchange which still identifies the urban way of life.

In recent years, however, the advent of shopping centers, with their dependence upon the automobile for accessibility, brought about a decline in the center. Shops with marginal profits caved in. Older merchants, rather than modernizing to stay competitive, retired early. The city fathers panicked and sold four-fifths of the park to a supermarket chain.

It's an old, old story. Decentralization in the form of cheap-land shopping centers (de-centers is more appropriate) with acres of black-top parking to tickle the fancies of two-car families have wrought economic ruin upon the established Central Business Districts; and instead of using their collective heads to fight the new competitors, the CBD merchants too often react like tract house owners to a blockbuster. They cut and run; or in the case of our suburb, they quickly dispensed with the only real weapon against the outside shopping threat which they possessed.

Today the little shops and cluster of civic buildings are grouped around an airplane hanger of a building, separated from it by the gray asphalt of a dusty parking lot. The architectural juxtaposition seems ludicrous; but even moreso, the forlorn strip of remaining park with its empty, broken benches and stunted, dirt-covered trees. The councilman was right. No one seems to use it. (The new supermarket has not proven to be the answer hoped for by the city fathers, and it too began to decline, leaving them to scratch their heads for another solution.)

The special meeting of the city council took no action on the park site proposition. That was several years ago. Today the lemon grove still stands undeveloped, awaiting the next building boom, the next plethora of cheaply built houses, and then the last open space within the inner city will be gone forever. Such a development could eventually bring up to 75 new taxpayers into the city. Councilmen understand taxpayers—if not the public. When their children look for a place to play, well, there is always the street.

INTRODUCTION

"It was a town of red brick, that would have been red had the smoke and ashes allowed it; but as matters stood, it was a town of black and red, like the painted face of a savage. It was a town of machinery and tall chimneys out of which interminable serpents of smoke trailed themselves forever and ever. It had a black canal in it and a river that ran purple with evil smelling dye, and vast piles of buildings where there was a rattling and trembling all day long, and where the pistons of steam engines worked monotonously up and down like the head of an elephant in melancholy madness. It contained several large streets, one very much like another, inhabited by people equally like one another, who went in and out at the same hours with the same sound upon the pavements, to do the same work, and to whom every day was the same as yesterday and tomorrow, and every year the counterpart of the last and the next."

Charles Dickens, *Hard Times*

PART 1
THE PARK THROUGH HISTORY

ONLY YESTERDAY

The American city is in trouble. The fear and anguish associated with urban life in United States today is known to all, and a popular theme from pulpit to picket, from reform politicians, chambers of commerce, and parent-teacher associations to purveyors of corruption, tenement landlords and welfare recipients. The great gray jungles, across the breadth of the land, offer opportunity and diversity—a chance to get rich. The city is just about the only place left to build an empire, or turn a quick profit. The city also offers its inhabitants filthy air to breathe, intolerable levels of noise, drab, colorless vistas and dangers—real dangers—of every conceivable dimension. The American city, as we know it, is dying.

How did it happen? Why is it that these great urban centers, from which the might of the nation was forged, have become so unlivable? The answers are sometimes lost in the rhetoric, which like New York's smog, swirls about the issues, choking the voices of reason and clouding the vision of hope. Causes and effects become confused, intertwined in the dialogue of blame. But the answers are there. At least the reasons—painful to accept because of the inescapable implications to the quality of American life those reasons suggest—but nevertheless discernable, even obvious.

The urban crisis in United States began a hundred years ago—a long time by American time reckoning. It was forged in the mills of industry by men of vision and determination who had found in 19th Century economic liberalism and unbounded American natu-

ral resources a combination of pure gold. Impatient to compete successfully with the more advanced markets of Europe, America's builders sacrificed her cities' rustic beauty and livability to commerce and industry, creating railroad terminals in the place of squares, and stockyards for parks, cutting across a city's heart, offending sight, smell and sound, degrading human life for the expedience of growth.

The destruction of the fabric of American cities by industry during this period was so complete that urban planners and historians are forced to go back to the preceding century, the premachine age, in order to find true American examples of constructive, imaginative urban planning. The New England green towns, with their carefully planned village squares and tree-lined avenues; the Spanish American settlements, which followed a precise formula for proper development of plaza, government structures and residential buildings; the early Southern towns, settled by Spanish, French and English colonists, with their broad stretches of public green, planned urban vistas which featured major public building and handsome walls for residential privacy and well being. Vestiges of 18th and early 19th Century urban planning remain today in Deerfield, Massachusetts, Annapolis, Santa Fe, Williamsburg, and parts of Savannah, Albuquerque and New Orleans. But these are not cities so much as museums—reconstructions, monuments to a long dead past. Sadly, the American visitors find them charming. These temporary excursions into the past amuse us when instead they should make us very, very, angry. Here, America, is our heritage! Here is what we gave away so quickly for expedience of growth. How much have we grown, then? How big have we become?

The 19th Century commercial-industrial wave brought employment to the cities and, hence, people in uncontrollable numbers. Open space was quickly eaten up by unplanned tenement housing. Factories sprang up without benefit of logic. Railroads, the new arteries to industry, gave nary an inch to logical planning, and accepted as their rightful place the very centers of the bursting, choking cities. Yet people continued to arrive, and the captains of industry found uses for this human fodder. Working hours stretched from dawn to dusk, children went to the mines and factories rather than to school, and entire families huddled throughout their lives in the shadows of the steel mill. The tenement earned its name.

Where no human qualities were able to develop, America's urban dwellers began to look elsewhere—at least those who were able—for the city's departed spirit. They found it eventually, with the aid of the automobile, on the fringes of urban development, in the new suburbs where in close proximity to real nature the park wasn't really needed—not by these escapists anyway. Thus the urban park concept, late in coming to American cities, was quickly circumvented in favor of the individual yard. The headlong surge toward private property, abetted by the unlivability of the inner city and the pioneer instinct to own land, shaped urban growth; and the amorphous, unplanned sprawl of free-wheeling suburban America spilling out over the rural landscape or leaping checkerboard-like to bargain sites was underway, leaving the urban core forgotten and despised. Here the new suburbanite would come to make his living but not his home. And here only the poor, the unemployed and the unwanted, by force of necessity, would remain.

How much of today's civic chaos is a result of an environment thus created? Central open space, or the lack of it, is both a result and a cause. These last hundred years have seen the shaping of American cities into industrial giants, and the lack of valid public open space is one result of that growth. What then, has this in turn caused? Commercial expedience still commands its way. In Los Angeles, for example, the elevated freeway systems are destroying neighborhood continuity and pedestrian scale just as the railroads dehumanized Cleveland nearly a century ago. The measure of any great civilization, according to John Ruskin, is its cities; and the measure of a city's greatness is to be found in the quality of its public spaces—its parks and squares. The fate of American cities must be reckoned with the fate of urban space. An oversimplification perhaps, but both ancient Athens and her Persian enemies as well recognized the significance of a central public space where free men might gather to discuss their affairs and their governments. Whether such a purely physical arrangement is a result or a cause of freedom can be argued, but certainly its steady decline in America must be a danger sign, a warning to those who would listen.

And what has been the fate of the city park? Ill-conceived, abused, misunderstood, the park concept is atrophying today because it remains static within a rapidly shifting urban crucible. And so, ironically, we are faced with trying to save something which has never really existed, or at best, never reached fruition in the American society. Better, we must try to create something which American urbanity has long hungered for but has never fully understood. We must create urban park systems, flexible in plan and dynamic in growth so as to better reflect shifting urban patterns. But primarily, we must come to understand the real meaning and purpose of the urban park—and, hence, the park system's potential value. Our parks are too few, too small, too remote. At best, they are islands of escape, separated from the surrounding city by major thoroughfares, drainage ditches and walls, rather than being integrated parts of a well-balanced urban scheme. They are, for the larger part, underdeveloped, badly organized and drab. The presence of pompous statues, cannons and plaques, and the absence of flowers, people and play tend to associate them with what *was* rather than what *is* or what *can be*. The parks tend to become memorials to the past—or someone's idea of the past—static anachronisms lost in rapidly changing surroundings.

The mania for private property in the United States has had its corollary—apathy or even disdain for public property. The word "taxpayers" is substituted for "public," as many a local politician has come to realize in order to accomplish civic programs. A taxpayer is a property owner and, therefore, entitled to a greater voice than the public in resolving city affairs. Any change in present levels of apathy must await the amalgamation of "taxpayers" and "public" into simply "people."

In spite of such widespread disregard for public well-being, and amidst the chaos of crumbling social foundations, can anything resembling constructive park planning be accomplished? While cities close their parks against social upheaval and racial unrest out of fear and hatred, let us plan new park systems, not as short-sighted do-gooders who would plant flowers on the highways, but while trying to understand the causes of urban unrest, and in concert with those who keep their faith in American cities, let us make a start.

For many urban dwellers, the city's only excuse for existence is a commercial one; and, as noted, they have long ago fled to the temporary safety of stratified suburbia. For those who choose to, or must remain behind, solid answers to urban salvation need to be found. Indeed, the future of the city will have to be determined by just such people. The intense and complicated problems of modern urban life will not be resolved in New Rochelle, Beverly Hills, or Webster Groves, but in the ghettoes and high-rise apartments of the unreconstructed downtowner. If he chooses in angry frustration to foul his nest as a first step toward changing existing urban patterns, then what will follow? It is the second step which urban designers should begin to prepare for now. And what should be the role of the city park? Can its structure be reshaped, its purposes reassessed to meet the needs of tomorrow's city? The parks of the past may offer some clues toward this endeavor. A look at urban history should emphasize the need to find new and more realistic answers. Perhaps the past remains the best resource in planning the future.

FRAGILE CONCEPTS AND A BEGINNING

During the first half of the 19th Century, a few years before it washed over the American shore, the industrial age plunged Europe into a binge of urban upheaval which threatened to sweep away all traces of agrarian economics and change the face of western cities forever.

While the advent of the machine age in Europe brought a new wealth in industrial invention—steel and glass structures, machine goods, power driven factories, and new colonial empires—it also brought the same overcrowded, unimaginatively conceived and hastily built tenements, loss of open space, uncontrolled pollution and unplanned growth which were to prove even more devastating to American cities a few decades later. Surveying the havoc wrought by industrial development in Britain's Midland cities and the levels of pollution carried by the Mersey and Severn Rivers, Patrick Geddes, a far-sighted English botanist turned city planner (and earlier day Paul Erlich) warned of the impending disaster—both organic and psychological—which would overtake our cities. Very few listened. But from the hazardous and depressing conditions born of this age, and from the smouldering grime of Victorian England, where industrial development was most advanced, came the rasping cry for social and physical reform in the cities—not from the elite and comfortable who benefited most from industrialization, nor to any great extent from enlightened intellectuals, but from the weary, oppressed masses of overworked and overcrowded public. Here the modern park concept was born.

Together with the labor union movement, and for much the same reason, the city park movement was a response—a hope for an improvement in the desperate living conditions which industrial expedience had wrought. Thus in the 1850's in London, Birmingham, Manchester, and other industrial centers of England there began to appear modest green patches, poorly designed and underdeveloped, and in most instances, bearing the identical name—Victoria Park.

But, significant to the changing tempo of the period, the royal parks of London already in existence in one form or another for centuries were soon to be transformed from private or semi-private parks completely to public parks—and it is these, together with the broad green commons, the traditional open spaces of English cities, which today form the basis of London's ample park system although none of these was originally intended to serve as such.

This then will prove to be the major characteristic of all of Europe's traditional city parks, since her cities developed into their present forms before man experienced industrial power and modern democracy. They share a past rich in the history of western progress, for it is in such parks that we encounter the evidence of western society's ancient beginnings, the strife of the middle ages, articulation of Renaissance humanism and haughty Baroque flamboyance. Here is found the wealthy and varied ancestry of public parks brought down to one level, one purpose, by modest, unprepossessing Victoria Park—and the 19th Century urban upheaval.

But rich as they might prove to be in history, these older parks and gardens are somewhat restrictive in contemporary use and future potential. The tight formality of the Luxembourg Gardens in Paris, the rigidity of Renaissance symmetry in general, and the careful protection of historic relics and design concepts make them less capable of meeting present and future recreational demands. While strolling through the Luxembourg Gardens or any of a number of Europe's historic estate parks, one is constantly reminded of a glorious past—and its inconsistency with today's park needs. Tucked in among the fountains, grand stairways and embroidery of formal plantings are found occasional sandboxes, swings and carousels struggling to secure a place of their own. The singular advantage of European parks over American counterparts should not, however, be overlooked. They exist. Would Luxembourg, Kensington and Borghese occur at all were it not for the privileged class and the 17th and 18th Century way of life which created them?

American cities are, by comparison, park poor since few such large, centrally located private estates ever existed. America's major city parks were, in almost every instance, developed from the beginning for public use.

The city parks of the western world owe their existence then to the creation of democratic institutions and, likewise, to the need to counter the urban environment of 19th Century industrialization. There is, however, an older heritage of civic space to reckon with; for while the full realization of public parks is little more than a century old, it is necessary to go back some 2,500 years to Classic Athens in order to discover the public park's conceptual origin—in the philosophy created by free men, which enabled public gathering at the town's center. Here within easy reach of all her citizens, that city, which we recognize as the crucible of democracy and individuality, undertook perhaps the noblest experiment in the long history of western town planning by creating

an open space in her very heart—a space devoted to the citizenry. Socrates taught here and nowhere else. Plato spent his formative years here. The news (as well as gossip) was disseminated here along with produce and exotic merchandise from far-off places. This large, central space, the size of two football fields laid side-by-side, was the *agora*. Born in Athens, it eventually became the

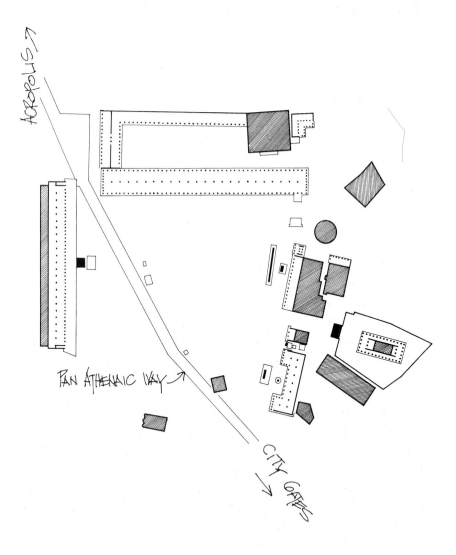

major identifying characteristic of most Greek cities of ancient times. It became the instrument for every kind of urban exchange, where one could observe athletes in training, get the latest news of local and distant occurences, listen to an expansion of the applications of democracy, and buy the ingredients for supper. This *agora*, unstructured in terms of precise design, dynamic insomuch as its physical dimensions were completely resultant upon its surrounding forces, became the focus of Athenian society and her political institutions. To attempt to define something of its importance by studying its archaeological remains (a favorite pastime of art historians) is folly. Even in its own time, the agora's strength lay in its ideals, not its design, and the less finite that design the more flexible and multifaceted its functions. As such, it is the ancestor in principle to the city park, the plaza, the market place, the campus, and the shopping centers of today. The village green of Colonial America is perhaps our most direct descendant of the classic agora, and as such represents another testimonial, in terms of physical planning, to the humanizing qualities of urban democracy. Its form somewhat uncertain, its function and values nonetheless clear to those who sought in America a greater measure of freedom, the green is perhaps the best example in later times of the application of this classic experiment. Therefore, we are better advised to refer to the *agora concept* than to its physical being, or to those rather pathetic, adored remnants in a city which today has so vastly misconstrued their meaning. It is the *agora concept* which planners of a modern democratic society must labor to rediscover and, hence, to recreate. Later under Roman occupation, the Athenian agora suffered a fate now old and familiar in the annals of city planning. It was cut up, filled in, structured and framed until no flexibility or significantly large space remained. Its center was littered with statuary, a huge theatre, temples and other such bric-a-brac which forever plaque urban open space. Thus from the example of the Athenian agora, western culture is left two legacies—one positive and one negative—in connection with the development and maintenance of open space in the cities. A lesson to those who would design, maintain, administrate or enjoy city parks and squares: Remember the *agora concept*—keep the Romans out!

THE REMNANTS OF STRUGGLE

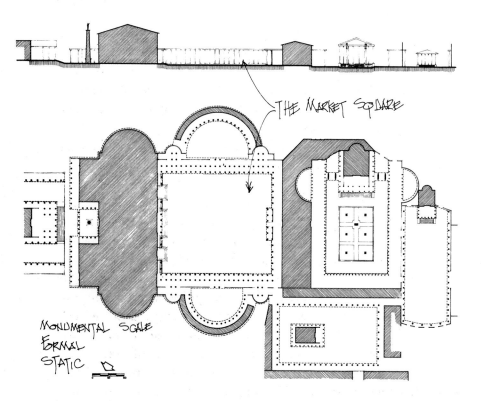

THE MARKET SQUARE

MONUMENTAL SCALE
FORMAL
STATIC

While the application of the city park concept derives from ancient democratic institutions, parks themselves have come into being from widely varied beginnings, usually unrelated to any such functions of rest and rejuvenation.

The Romans left little beyond a further expansion and elaboration of Greek themes. The near total destruction of their architectural remains presupposes little hope otherwise, and today a stroll through the forum's ruins is about as close to a park experience as can be expected. It is well to point out, however, that any parklike qualities with which the forum and the Palatine Hill are imbued, Lord Byron notwithstanding, derive from the ruins and not the Roman originals. It is the overgrowth of vines and grasses amongst the broken rubble, the volunteer shrubbery and broad crowned Italian pines that produce the nostalgic beauty, as appealing to 20th Century tourists as it was for 19th Century romantic poets. Modern Roman planners, understanding their value in more than historic terms, are careful to preserve these places in an otherwise auto clogged city.

To a greater extent, the physical remains of a hard way of life in cities of the middle ages have come down through the centuries to become a part of today's city park system. Parks deriving from medieval fortifications are rather commonplace in European cities. They are generally the result of a natural morphology of urban growth and development, beginning in a fearsome, anarchic age when the selection of a castle or town site necessarily included consideration for defense. Such defenses as hills, riverbends, islands, as well as moats and elaborate wall systems rendered these strongholds impractical and inhibitive to trade in later, safer times.

To survive in a competitive, commercial Europe, considerable physical change was involved. The image of the city had to shift completely from remote and unattainable to open and inviting. Such an example is found at Edinburgh where a great, natural rise above the Firth of Forth gave early settlers of this region both a port and a potential stronghold. While the heights upon which the castle was built were sufficiently steep to insure against attack by enemies, inconvenience and lack of comfort made such strongholds less than agreeable to their inhabitants; and thus in later periods, the center of growth in Edinburgh shifted to the foot of the hill and especially to the harbor. We see these patterns of growth repeated all over western Europe, from the 10th to the 16th Century, as commerce gradually replaces defendability as the major criterion in a town's development. Those towns which survived in this later commercial age were the ones which were located at natural seaports, on navigable rivers, on the great inland trade routes, or on rich, arable plains. The accident of nature, such as a steep rise in the landscape, which had been the primary consideration for settlement, often remained an unnecessary curiosity in the center of an expanding metropolis. Thus at somewhat different times in their histories, Paris (an island in a river), Luxembourg (a bend in a steep gorge, giving three naturally protected sides), Copenhagen (an island in the sea), and Venice (a man-made island), like Edinburgh, were forced by commercial necessity to expand beyond their original, natural defenses. While the two characteristics, defendability and productivity, call upon entirely different natural bases, they were, nevertheless, fundamental to medieval survival towns. Eventually when the fortified stronghold was no longer of use to the growing town, it fell to neglect—a relic. But by this time, the physical structure of the town had usually been determined, and the relic was irrevocably a part of the structure. The steep slopes of Edinburgh forbade urban development and the castle stood isolated, forgotten although remaining central. Eventually and after a sufficient passage of time to render them historic, these old fortresses were restored and thus became commercially productive themselves as tourist attractions. The inevitable final chapter is thus written—the restored structure becomes a museum and the surrounding steep slopes, moats and revetments having defied destruction for centuries, become parks.

Parks which have thus evolved are certain to vary considerably in shape and structure as their origins varied. They tend to be well located as explained but suffer from obvious disadvantages. After all, they are vestigial, or at best inherited from another age rather than designed to meet the needs of this one; and physically, they are *transitional,* occupying what is often the steep and rugged terrain between stronghold and city below.

At Nurnburg, Salzburg and Lisbon, for example, the situation is practically identical: A steeply inclined natural rise surmounted by a fortress, a commercially adaptable surrounding area or port; and today acting as a transition between the two elements, a steeply contoured, limited-use city park best appreciated by tourists and hiking enthusiasts.

Water was also a means of defense in the early middle ages, leading to the location of fortresses on islands (Paris, Mont St. Michel), on promentories (Orvietto), at river bends (Luxembourgville), etc. Where such sites were found to be commercially valuable, especially in the case of developing trade routes, the same urban morphology occurs with certain advantages of accessibility in view of potential parks. Luxembourg-ville is surrounded on three sides by a deep stream-filled ravine, a natural and highly successful means of defense calling for protection on only one side. Today the ravine acts as a *belt-park* lending charm and scale to the tightly structured city; but a series of bridges was necessary in order to overcome the original purpose in choice of site.

In some instances where natural defenses were not significant, defenders were forced to rely on their own resources to a greater extent, leading to considerable variation and refinement of the wall in combination with earthworks, wards, moats, etc. Where a system of walls of sufficient width existed, the remains of such today may lend themselves to development as parks. At Lucca, the restoration of walls and revetments has resulted in a sort of ring park. Centrally located and faithfully adapted from the design of the revetments, the park appears as a unifying agent and spatial relief for the somewhat crowded medieval interior. Lucca is today the only city in Europe with its ancient walls intact. While the old battlements act primarily as a park, they also provide the means for a ring-road upon which the higher speed traffic moves. This elevated road, completely encircling the city, performs as a freeway, even providing off-ramps down to the city below. Rather than crisscrossing Lucca with a plethora of surface traffic, the ring-road on the old walls gives easy access to all parts of the city without destructive penetration. It seems a lesson of which Los Angeles, as well as all other cities contemplating the construction of elevated freeways, could have made use. In Copenhagen two defensive belts were constructed, an inner late medieval system which protected the castle and harbor by means of a complex arrangement of earthwork and moats, and an 18th Century system on the outskirts. While neither proved to be of any real practical use, today the remnants of each form the basis of the city's park system. While the inner "moat parks" are rather small, they afford green space in the most intensely commercial part of the city, including even the harbor area. But like all parks which are limited to the area of ancient defenses, severe limitations in use exist. Even Lucca's circle of green is essentially a dimunitive green belt and does not possess sufficient depth for major park development. Many European towns and cities which still possess the remnants of medieval citadels likewise maintain the open green esplanade which once separated castle from surrounding structures for protective purposes. These grassy stretches, now tree-lined in many cases, have performed as public promenades for centuries and to this day remain all too often the only semblance of public park in many auto-clogged old world towns.

On the other hand the English commons, great stretches of natural land left undeveloped through the centuries because of poor drainage conditions, must by counted today amongst the finest of inherited city parks. Certainly the commons represent one of the greatest examples of open space heritage from the Middle Ages.

THE HERITAGE OF POWER

Beginning in Northern Italy, with the sudden rise of a wealthy merchant class and the reawakening fervor for classic themes of ancient Rome, there developed a garden style imminently reflective of the times. As an outgrowth of Renaissance values, the 16th and 17th Century Italian gardens often described even more closely the concepts of humanism—a rationale in spatial terminology which praises the accomplishments and potential of man.

By using nature's materials—water, gravel, trees, shrubs, and stone—in an unnatural, geometric way, the Renaissance garden architects clearly demonstrated man's assault of and eventual dominion over nature. It is a victory which enjoys little appreciation or understanding in our modern technological society, which has seen nature become the victim of a shortsighted, wasteful desecrator—Humanism's progeny. The gardens of the Renaissance are therefore scorned today for what they once represented. This is, however, an unfair condemnation. It was not 16th Century Renaissance man who spoiled his environment. For him nature was a haughty, relentless master. Together with religion, these two imposing forces shaped and limited his life. Humanism—a blend of men's achievements in literature, science and art—returned to him an image of himself which he had lost since ancient times. Geometric garden design, because it offered no practical function while using nature's own materials was the logical choice for the celebration of Humanism—and the victory of the human spirit. Such gardens reflected an extension of man's freedom of thought and thus remained passive, visual, and contemplative in use. As a result, the rush towards Humanism proved too much for even the church to resist; and the role of Christianity in the 16th Century is succinctly inscribed in history by the architecture of cathedrals and villas—both humanistically conceived and both ably serving the same earthly masters. The direct, rational logic implied in Humanism eventually proved detrimented to the church's philosophic structure which was unable to refute or resist its appeal. As wealthy merchants achieved control over city-states and finally the papacy itself, the destiny of the church in the 16th Century was assured. The legacy of the worldly popes—the Reformation—was certain to follow.

Despite the later political and religious upheavals blowing through the 16th Century, the revolution in spatial order wrought by the philosophies of Humanism continued to develop almost unchallenged by the fervor and torment of this momentous century. Precise mathematical interpretations of order and balance,

13

the concepts of humanistic rationale, if lacking a sense of human spirit, continued to be the accepted approach to environmental design. The ultimate in self-imposed order had been reached in ancient, pagan Rome, with the Pantheon and the Basilica of Constantine. Now we are to see it again, imposed by St. Peters in Christian Rome, and later in the royal palace and gardens of Versailles. Ordered precision without the involvement of human scale or human spirit eventually diminished the force of Renaissance space, giving rise to the organic vibrancy of the Baroque. Renaissance space and spirit had thus run their course. The Reformation, both Catholic and Protestant, replaced it with a new spirit of mysticism not unlike the Gothic. In those areas of Europe which remained Catholic—specifically Italy, Spain and Southern Germany—the church and its architecture reflect the spirit of victory over materialism and a separation from the secular pursuits· of their predecessors.

Throughout the 16th and 17th Centuries, garden design re-

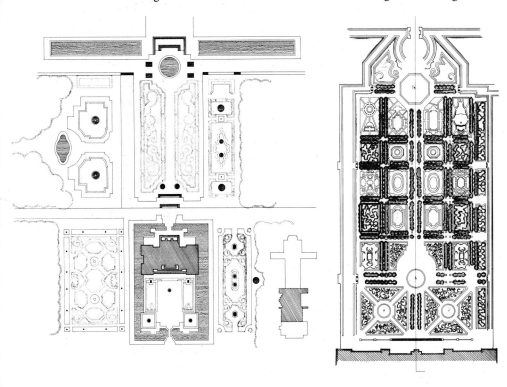

mained meticulously balanced, geometrically ordered and spatially inflexible. The garden architects of Florence and Rome best understood the functions and limitations of the style and kept their works singular of purpose, visually direct and relatively small. The rugged hillside sites they selected added immeasurably to the effectiveness of the humanistic themes and man's apparent supremacy. The steepness of the site provided a view from the top, a most necessary consideration if one were to grasp the full context and meaning implied by such an arrangement of geometric forms. Here one commanded an imposing view of cascading waterways, bubbling statuary and dramatic fountains set amongst diamonds and rectangles of boxed shrubbery and pleached trees. Ordered masses of deep green cypress could highlight a lovely nude standing in bright contrast to her surroundings, while columns of shaped evergreens directed one's attention to distant vistas. The success which was achieved in Italy, with smallness of scale and bold changes in elevation, was lost in the vast, flat extensions of the theme elsewhere in Europe. Humanism had, after all, established a sense of scale in the garden. Man felt himself to be mathematically and spiritually the measure of his surroundings. Here he could establish linkage between his mind, his world and the cosmos itself. The stars thus became only a measurable extension of his environment. On the other hand, the seemingly endless stretches of flat parterres and arrow-straight vistas, with their elaborately embroidered borders, express primarily the single-minded, aristocratic pride of royalty. At Versailles especially and also Vaux-le-Vicomte and Fontainebleau, royal pride echoes like a trumpet across the broad, geometric plain.

Today the inflexibility of design and purpose, the remote locations, and the generally small size make the typical Italian Renaissance gardens impractical as potential city parks. Thus the Villa Lante and the Villa d'Este near Rome, the period's most famous gardens, remain tourist attractions preserved for history. The Boboli Gardens, near the center of Florence have the advantage of size and location; but this sprawling geometric maze, like those grand, haughty gardens of France, meets few of the complex requisites of the modern city park. It is difficult enough to renovate or restore old masterpieces—especially gardens. It is far more of a task to modify them so as to meet modern park needs without serious damage to the original design. Parks, however, are for the living, and uncompromising anachronisms may prove to be impossible to live with. Sacred cows, it is said, make good hamburgers.

By the end of the 17th and throughout the 18th Century, a new concept in private gardens was developed by the powerful aristocracies—the great estate. Foregoing the tight geometry of humanistic contemplation, the new masters of society evoked individual success rather than the superiority of man—a concept certain to be better grasped—and obtained large holdings, often thousands of acres outside the noisy, filthy cities. Taking a lead from such 16th Century personages as Henry VIII and Francis I, the wealthy houses of Europe created great hunting parks and wooded retreats, large enough and at a sufficient distance to be safe from the increasing urban discontent. It was to be these anti-urban royal reserves which would become the great public parks of the 19th Century. The expansion of the cities eventually brought them into the urban picture; and the advent of broad based democratic institutions, achieved by the blood and sweat of mankind, made them at last available to public use.

The most significant characteristic of the great estate, however, proved to be the design concept itself. Emanating from England, where a traditional love for the natural landscape had forestalled a general acceptance of the Italian garden, designers of the early 18th Century began to experiment with "naturalizing." Influenced by the symbolic asymmetry of Chinese and Japanese gardens, the English designers feverishly sought new design bases for their explorations. In addition to religion and oriental philosophy, music, poetry, and even the 18th Century landscape paintings of Corot and other romanticists became the new foundations for landscape design. During this frenetic period of exploration which could be called the foolish age of landscape design, all sorts of theatrics were indulged in—artificial volcanoes were built, wild animal preserves were created, idyllic scenes from the orient were staged, as well as plays from Greek mythology, complete with nymphs and satyrs who were hired to dart nakedly across the paths of delighted guests. Roman ruins were constructed, especially triumphal arches, bits of aqueduct and temples of Venus, a number of which can still be found in English parks and estates. Dripping grottoes were popular, along with artificial caves where hired hermits came to reside. It was for garden designers, an age of conflict, filled with artless nostalgia and poetic nonsense, while at the same time being in open rebellion against the geometric gardens which had dominated the scene for two centuries.

Eventually the master of the style arrived in the person of Lancelot Brown. Called "Capability" by his detractors, Brown swept the English estates clear of their Italian and later romantic design schemes. A most prolific landscape architect, he brought a maturity to the style which was soon to have an influence throughout the continent, as well as the United States. Today the English natural style of the late 18th Century remains the dominant design element in most of the traditional city parks of Europe and the United States. This is primarily because of its adaptability to large areas and its lingering influence on estate design at the time of the 19th Century Industrial Revolution.

Many of Europe's large city parks retain major aspects of their previous grandeur. Sacred cows, like Luxembourg Gardens and Jardin de Plantes, remain curiously stuffy amongst their less formal left bank surroundings. The Tuilleries Gardens, however, seem appropriate to the scale and formality of the center of Paris, reminding one of the lost Palace and earlier glory.

While strolling or driving through Rome's Villa Borghese, one is never allowed to forget the power and nobility of that once powerful family. Today the Borghese home is an art museum, and the ample hunting grounds and gardens have been converted to public use. The romantic imagery remains, nevertheless, in a thousand vestiges of past glory. Broken and crumbly, these remnants of a Baroque past, like the classic ruins of the forum, add to the city's unique quality of timelessness. Amongst them creep the practical, if prosaic artifacts of more recent times serving as reminders of the need for flexibility and space in that beautiful, crowded park.

Truly most of Europe's old established parks are former estates. In London alone, Richmond, St. James's, Kensington–Hyde, Green, Greenwich and Bushy parks all result from royal hunting grounds. The Villas Ada and Doria-Pamphili in Rome are rather curious examples of great estates in transition to becoming public parks. Regent's Park in London is another example of transition of a sort. Designed by John Nash for the Prince Regent (later to become George IV), it was intended to serve the ruling family in much the same manner as traditional estates of the

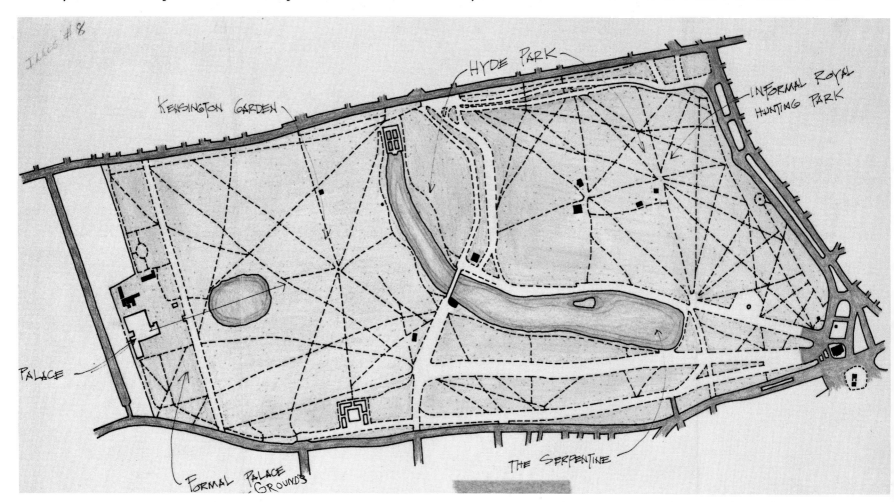

times. Nash, however, envisioned the estate in terms of its *surroundings* rather than of the planned palace. He *reversed* the visual direction by framing the estate with handsome terraces of classic design. These housed the wealthy and prominent citizens of London and provided them with a magnificent view *across the park*—basically the same functional relationship as exists between New York's Central Park and its surrounding frame of apartment buildings. Though not yet a public park, Nash's visual orientation represented a new concept in estate design—and the prince never built his palace there.

It should be noted that this concept had been developed earlier but on nowhere near so great a scale. A prototype of the framed park exists in Paris in the Place des Vosges. With perhaps greater foresight than the Prince Regent, Henry IV of France planned from the outset to occupy quarters within the surrounding residential framework of this great square. Though never a genuine public park, Place des Vosges should, nevertheless, be recognized as a truly ingenious concept, some 200 years prior to Nash's breakthrough at Regent's Park. The Place des Vosges is perhaps better noted as the original model for the many semi-private, or key parks found throughout London, Boston and New York. Like the later residential square of 18th Century England, only the immediate residents of the Place des Vosges had access to its grounds.

By the end of the 18th Century the search for a more careful integration of mass and open space in the city was achieved in Bath, England—a success rarely improved upon to this day.

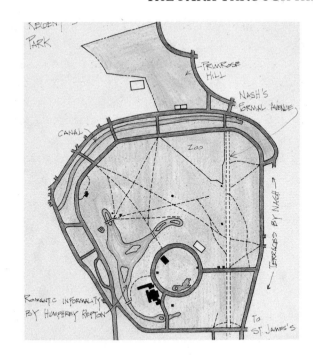

ROYAL CRESCENT, CIRCUS

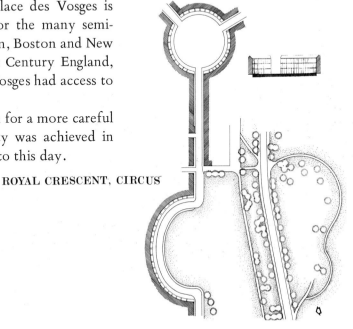

THE VIRTUES OF URBANITY

Napoleon III and Georges Haussmann, combining power and vision, completely overhauled the central structure of Paris in the early 19th Century and in so doing changed the daily habits of Parisians and strongly influenced urban patterns throughout the western world. Born of empire and its ensuing grandeur, the new shape of Paris reflected the power and pride of old, together with a new regard for its citizenry, a combination which has resulted in a lasting love affair between Parisians and their city; and the love affair remains intact.

The vast proportions of 19th Century Paris might have lost all context of human scale (as happened earlier at Versailles) were it not for the "promenades"—the tree-lined, formally structured sidewalks of Paris. Here amongst the fountains, floral displays, avenues of clipped horse chestnuts, the benches, and gravel walks the people of Paris took their Sunday afternoon stroll, or drank their coffee in tree-shaded cafes. Before Haussmann and Napoleon III scraped centuries of clutter off the face of Paris—an undertaking which took about thirty years—the city had been choking in its own accumulation of historic flotsam—narrow, crooked streets and imposing problems for health, fire and police protection, let alone services. After completion of the Haussmann plan, many of the medieval streets and buildings remained—as they do today—but Paris almost overnight became the most modern city in the world. Parisians poured into her streets and new sidewalk cafes, as artists and foreign dignitaries flocked to the city to discover for

themselves her newly made delights. The Industrial Age had brought pollution and chaotic planning to English cities; while, at the same time, Paris was becoming the "city of lights."

The promenade parks of the city were the basis for the city's physical park system connecting by ribbons of green the old and new gardens, the great avenues, and the historic monuments. From west to east, a visual connection of truly magnificent proportions had been effected, starting from the Bois de Boulogne along the Champs Elysees through the Arc de Triomphe to the Place de la Concorde—a major pivotal point—through the Tuilleries and on through a series of interlinking green spaces to the receptacle of the Louvre's Pavilion d'Horloge. Beyond the Louvre, the continuity of spatial order carries visually at least as far as the Place Bastille, where the *grande plan* breaks down into the characteristic jumble of the eleventh arrondissement. The only remnants of the fearsome old prison are found in the painted cobblestones which indicate the site of its long departed foundation; but the personality of the Bastille area still reflects much of the 18th Century genre atmosphere. (Victor Hugo's home is only a stone's throw away in the Place des Vosges.)

Another axis running north-south moves down Avenue St. Germaine, incorporating Luxembourg Gardens on its way, crosses the major urban axis at the Ile de la Cité and continues north, though less distinctly, to Sacre Couer. This simple crossing of axial vistas greatly strengthens the internal organization of the city and remains today a civic concept of major significance amongst western cities.

Although formal and sedate in nature, the new parks, planned during the Haussmann epoch, reflect the popularity on the continent of the *jardin anglais*—the English Natural style developed by Lancelot Brown in the previous century. Thus Bois de Boulogne, Bois Vincennes and Buttes-Chaumont, to mention three, were planned by Haussmann at the particular request of the emperor, who had long admired London's Hyde Park.

The 19th Century brought us little in the way of architectural innovation, and Paris is no exception; but there remains a striking uniqueness about this city, where so high a degree of planning success was achieved with warmed over architectural techniques. And then, of course, nearer to the close of the century, a delightfully original, if perhaps shallow, design style began to emerge which was soon to make Paris the giddy, self-conscious "mod" center of Europe. Art Nouveau affected every aspect of style-setting Paris, from typeface to architecture, which might be seen to include under its umbrella much of the artificial charm that persists in Buttes-Chaumont Park today. There one still finds the concrete logs and branches, the poetic bridges, artificial naturalness and romantic settings. Nearby, as well as in other parts of the city, are still seen the characteristic lighthearted "metro" signs and stations which were on hand to inaugurate the turn of the century underground system, furthering Paris' claim to being the most advanced city of the world. The metro today, with its rubber-tired carriages and renovated underground stops, is still a style leader in that department; while similarly the redesigned *Parc Floral* in the Bois de Vincennes and other park renovations throughout the city are keeping Paris abreast of most European and American cities in up-dating park design to meet today's needs.

Design often lags behind the functioning of social order like the thunder following a lightning flash. That is to say, style is a reflection of its times and not their creator. Certainly the origina-

tive genius of the men who create the great works of their times is not to be denied them. It is through their skill and imagination that the social, political and religious values under which they labor and draw inspiration are made to bear fruit and offer testimony of themselves for the edification of those who follow. But even the most individualistic, the most iconoclastic of the creative breed would be hard pressed to develop an art form which does not speak for its own times. The reflective nature of art, plus the period of time necessary for maturation of an art form produce this time lag. Thus tiny skirts appear as an artistic product of permissiveness and liberation. Later, women in the same tiny skirts are seen to be fighting what shortened hemlines have apparently come to represent—sexual objectivity. Likewise during the greater part of the 16th Century, the established church was under attack from outside, as well as within, by a host of reformers. But it was not until the middle of the 17th Century that a new church style—one that reflected the labors of the Catholic reformers—had matured. So it has been with the development of city parks.

The 18th Century's brief flirtation with romantic themes and their consequent nostalgic spatial interpretations outlasted the age of reason and, in the design of parks, brought an air of elegance and rural aristocracy into the turmoil of the 19th Century's vigorous industrial growth. An overdue need for public green space, combined with the Englishman's traditional love of country life, help to explain the acceptance of bucolic themes, hopelessly out of date and out of context. Only the larger city parks managed to contain the 18th Century design philosophy of Lancelot Brown and others with any degree of integrity; and so Hyde Park and Regent's Park helped to form the conceptual base for Victoria Park and the other 19th Century Industrial Age parks to follow.

Victoria Park and the Paris plan are contemporaries. London did make a somewhat feeble attempt to capture some of Paris' new magic, as attested to by the construction of straight, tree-lined Pall Mall, and the Victoria Embankment—an unsuccessful copy of Paris' development along the Seine River. Victoria Park in terms of design never amounted to much; but as a new concept depicting popularly based informal park usage, it helped to change the social habits and physical structure of western cities, especially those in their formative periods like Stockholm, Hamburg, Copenhagen, Stuttgart, and most American cities.

The 19th Century city park, for all its nostalgic dependence upon design themes developed the century before, is nevertheless a cornerstone in the concept of the public city park. Of all the squares and other open spaces occurring in 19th Century English cities, those which developed as a response to pollution, noise and overcrowding in working class neighborhoods best represent the movement which produced the great American city parks in the last half of the century.

The residential squares of London represent a different purpose and period in history. Dating from the early 18th Century, their original design basis probably came from the simply structured, green squares of medieval Cambridge and Oxford. Like the larger parks, these squares suffered redesign in the nostalgic manner of the late 18th and early 19th Century. Today some of them (Russell Square) reflect a newer, contemporary design scheme, while others (Leicester Square, Victoria Square) retain the concepts of the nostalgic era. Grosvenor Square, exclusive of the Roosevelt Memorial and accompanying walks, is reminiscent of the earlier form of English collegiate squares. Likewise the key parks—those semi-private parks and playgrounds available only for the use of the surrounding apartments—have had less to do with broadening the democratic processes or encouraging public exchange in the manner of the open city park. However, Grosvenor, Leicester and especially the Bloomsbury area squares of 18th Century London undoubtedly influenced the development of the systematic green squares of Savannah and Philadelphia, and as such became forerunners of the American City Park movement.

It has been said that Englishmen, as a rule, rather dislike having to live in the city, preferring village and countryside. If

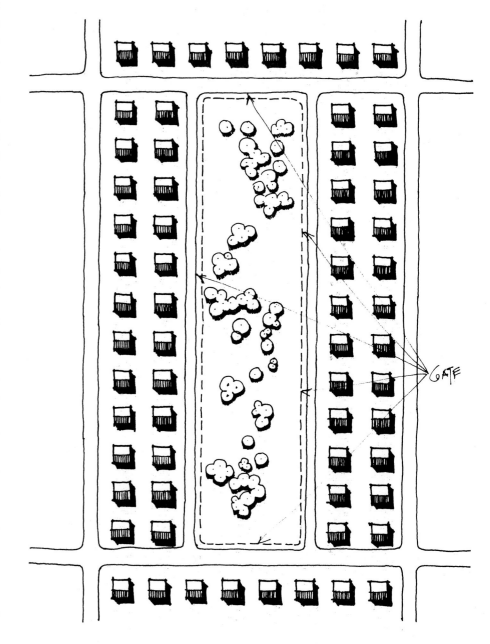

true, it might explain why English cities generally lack a sense of urban scale and continuity. The profusion of parks and green spaces suggests not so much good urban organization and balance as it suggests *retreat*. Just the opposite of Paris' system of *linking green corridors,* London's parks are mostly unrelated forests of escape—a place to hide from the ills of city life for those who, because of reasons of livelihood, are forced to live there. A notable exception is the attempt, though largely unsuccessful, by John Nash to establish linkage from Regent's Park to St. James's Park, and thus to bring some spatial continuity to the disassociated parts of the city. Most Londoners today profess to love their city; but this affection usually embraces historic events, quaintness, individual buildings or squares and, of course, parks. Rarely will a Londoner rave about the magnificence of the city's plan, its broad boulevards, its total sense of urbanity.

Thus it is apparent that the retreat park is a result of, and not a solution to, civic ills. The concept of a retreat park is in itself a confession of disdain for urbanism. This isn't to say that relief from congestion, noise and all of the general conditions of city life, good and bad, isn't desirable in the form of proper balance. But an attempt to achieve balance in the complex variables of a city's structure should not be interpreted as a seeking of means to escape. The park and the city are not in balance. No attempt to improve a city's park system, in quantity or quality, can of itself alone hope to overcome or even balance an entire city of generally negative character.

THE AMERICAN RESPONSE

The English Natural style, as applied to city park design, was readily accepted on the other side of the Atlantic without debate, or allowing for any period of critical analysis. While developing many significant and unique characteristics of a social and political nature, New Englanders nevertheless relied on the old world for its physical structure during the formative years of nationhood. Even the rather immature style of the *"gardenesque period,"* that tasteless turn of the century importation which featured floral clocks, half moons in the lawn, green houses in the front yard and keep-off-the grass signs, bringing to the American civic scene most of the characteristics of the English experience from 18th Century nostalgia to 19th Century trivia—as well as a very positive and lasting sense of belonging. In the years ahead, during rapid industrial expansion and self-centered commercial exploitation, the tradition of civic green space was to become the most steadfast means by which city land was obtained and held for park development. The European, and especially English tradition, was the basis for design, as well as establishment of the city park in the United States; but the nostalgic charm of romanticism didn't always fit well into the tight rectangles dictated by American cities' gridiron street patterns.

One American who managed to cope with the difficulties of rectangular street systems, as well as local animosity for public institutions, was Frederick Law Olmsted. While traveling through England, Olmsted came to understand and respect the need for large tracts of public green space, laid out in a generally natural style so as to accent physical contrasts with the rapidly developing cities. He came to grips with the problems relevant to translation of the English Natural style into the restrictive framework of the American gridiron city and successfully transposed many dumps, gravel pits and urban wastelands into this country's first planned city parks.

Given the awkwardness of a rectangular frame, Olmsted's designs called for a sufficiently large site in order to carry out the transition to curvilinear forms and, at the same time, provide relief from the surrounding city scope. Olmsted was a visionary as well as a skillful designer and anticipated the rapid growth of American cities, which today enjoy the benefits of his farsightedness through the realization of his large, well located city parks.

Forms that tend to duplicate natural line are not as forceful in themselves as the more easily perceived geometric shapes and, therefore, require broadening and repetition of their principle motifs in order to be assertive. This requires size. Nothing seems more pathetic in park design than the "wavy line" concept imposed on a small green rectangle. The other concern Olmstead mastered was circulation. Realizing the need to route heavy pedestrian traffic into and through the park, he thoroughly tested the "natural" design's ability to carry wide walks and direct access. In Central Park, Olmsted, while proving the ease and naturalness of circulation which was never very well developed in the earlier English estates, carried it one step farther. He separated pedestrian and vehicular circulation in the park completely, without impeding either, by planning a system of underpasses for foot traffic. So well conceived was Central Park in terms of adequate size and circulation that, one-hundred years after its original design and in the face of shifting external forces and a growing population, it has not required a major conceptual change or uplifting. The problems which plague Central Park today are not of its making.

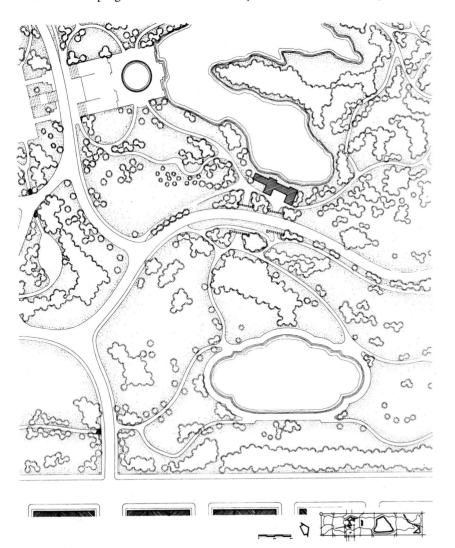

In the design of Central Park, Prospect Park and other large parks of Eastern and Southern cities, Olmsted established the English Natural style as the basis for city park design in America. By recognizing the purposes of the city park and altering the style to accommodate the needs of urban life, he helped to make the large, centrally located park a contrasting rather than a nonconforming aspect of American city life.

The second major contribution to city park development made by Olmsted was perhaps even more significant than his far reaching approach to design. This involved his life long struggle on behalf of Central Park to prevent commercial intrusion and land grabbing private development. Encroachment on park property has been a real and constant threat throughout this country's recent history. Olmsted was perhaps the first major figure to stand up and fight Tammany Hall politicians and greedy profiteers who would cash in on the park's lovely setting while, at the same time, diminishing the park by their actions. Parasitical developers still exist to threaten parks and open space in our cities; but because of Olmsted who made it his life's work to awaken city officials and people in general to the dangers of encroachment, the parks remain. It is for the followers of Olmsted to update, renovate, maintain and enlarge the parks—or see them atrophy into unused, dried up curiosities. When a park reaches that stage, even Olmsted would be hard pressed to save it. The almost slavish imitation of European design concepts continued, however, to haunt the American urban environment generally. The two great turn-of-the-century expositions in Chicago (1892-1893) and St. Louis (1904) attest to this, as witnessed by their dependence on neo-classic and Gothic-Victorian architecture, and both romantic and classic siting. At this same time, nevertheless, the hope for a unique and truly responsible American urban environment was being created in Chicago by such pioneers of civic design as city planner, Daniel Burnham, landscape architect, Jens Jensen, and architect, Louis Sullivan. Europeans visiting the two expositions recognized, in the works of such men, the emergence of American architectural independence, even before America did. It remained only for the far-sighted American designers of the 20th Century to complete the break. To a large degree, however, despite the better efforts of such pioneer landscape architects as Jensen and Olmsted, city park design continued to stumble along in pastoral escapism. Too often the park failed to create any link with the city. Indeed, for the most part, park design turned inward, like wagon trains under Indian attack, remaining "escapist" in purpose and design. Olmsted's Central Park reflects this characteristic, which amounts to a dissatisfaction on his part with the dynamic and imposing character of the immediate surroundings.

If Olmsted can be criticized—as he has been—for reflecting in his design of Central Park an escapist quality, Frank Lloyd Wright's Guggenheim Museum—facing the park—is likewise taken to task for ignoring its surroundings. Wright and Olmsted were both reacting to the same problem—dissatisfaction with the enclosing agent. The different methods used in dealing with this dissatisfaction again underscore the sublime, receptive nature of the park. Primarily a void in search of a frame, it can't ignore or outshoulder its surrounding masses. The quality of parks, as well as all open spaces, is dependent upon the overall character and amenities expressed by the city proper, and especially its immediate framework.

In criticizing Olmsted's escapist philosophy in Central Park it should be noted that he was responding to causes and reactions which he had observed in England, prior to his designing of Central Park. The broadening of democratic principles and functions taking place in the manufacturing cities toward the middle of the century, and the vehement protestations being made by and for the laboring classes in order to induce government and the powerful manufacturers to insert a bit of beloved rural countryside into the smoky foundryscape of the midlands' factory towns, collaborated in producing a neo-Romantic form of park design. The crowded poor had longed for the quiet village life which most of them had only recently been forced to quit in order to find work

in the new industrial centers. They wanted walks, picnics on Sunday, a bit of grass on a sunny spring day, and trees to break the harsh, angular monotony which sprawled and clanked about them.

In observing conditions of urban life in such towns Olmsted must have recognized the escapist theme as the very essence of city park design. Borrowing from the works of Joseph Paxton, J.C. Loudon and other contemporary park designers, he successfully transplanted England's park philosophy into America's bustling gridiron cities—and eliminated as well the plethora of Romantic vestiges which continued to plague his English contemporaries.

His American followers frequently, however, lacked his foresight. In numerous examples over the United States, the escapist park remains the overriding rule in city park design—along with the generally unrewarding habit of political-historical romanticizing. Unfortunately, the emphasis of romanticism and escapism in later American parks has resulted primarily in a clutter of military and idyllic memorabilia, together with an almost total lack of any comprehensive and efficient functional organization. The method by which many city parks in America have come into existence is by dedication as living memorials. Such parks are seen to be not so much recreational places for the living as memorials to the dead. And sadly enough, design, facilities and programs for further development often reflect this spirit. The image of the neighborhood park—a centrally placed military statue on a high pedestal (on or off horse) overlooking a couple of acres of unkempt grass and a few stunted trees—is readily called to mind by most people. Together with the nostalgic park of lagoons, little bridges and swans, one begins to feel that the "escapist" park is likely to become a never-never land into which one can pass through the looking glass from the real world of ugliness and cacophony.

For the unreconstructed Romantic, such a picture of swans, lagoons, heroes and nymphs may remain irresistible; but the realist, new concepts in park development are clearly needed. Within the grand manner of Luxembourg Gardens, urchins sail tiny boats in the majestic central basin, or play in new concrete sand pits, which have been shoehorned into the statue-lined formality of the Observatoire. The myriad examples of make-do situations, in so many traditional parks, point up the mounting pressures being placed on them in our rapidly changing urban society. Throughout history, the design of city parks has lagged behind contemporary urban achievements—always representing past values as though nostalgia were a criteria for park design. A systematic restructuring of city parks must be drawn from the social fabric of today's urban conditions—with plenty of elbow room for the future growth and activities not even imagined today. (After all, did the planners of Central Park envision the love-in, the go-kart, the 40-hour week?) Today's urban iconoclasm points the way toward a potential renaissance of the city. The efforts of our children will astound us if we give them a chance.

Historic usage has been responsible for preserving large tracts of land and creating so many of the great estates, which have resulted in our present park systems. The whims and cliches of light hearted aristocracy, the moats and battlements, the straight lines of the humanist and the wavy line of the naturalist, the purity of Olmsted's farsightedness and the haughtiness of Louis XIV's single-mindedness, the wisdom, frivolity, ugliness and beauty of our own western past are bound side by side—frozen in time between the fountains and laurels, walls and pillars, gravel and grass of our urban green. Today they are making tomorrow's design history in the parks of Stockholm and Amsterdam, in the new towns of Great Britain, and the new architecture of Italy.

And what of America? Will History write her off in the last half of the 20th Century as the technocracy that created smog, the slurb, strip-commercial, bedroom communities, stratified neighborhoods and trailer towns? We must find ourselves as a people or perish as a culture, and the city park may well be the best place to start. It is, after all, a reflection of the character of our urban past, as well as a portrait of our present. Great cultures have required leisure time in order to ripen. The great park is both a product of and a stimulus to cultural enrichment, and can provide the base for expanding cultural awareness in United States if its role is understood and supported.

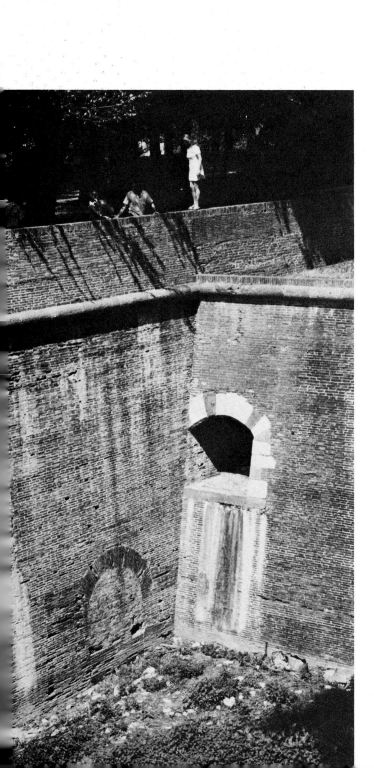

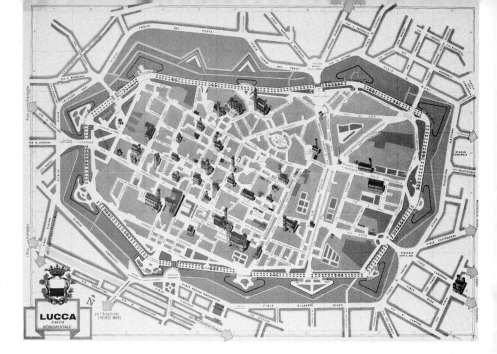

Lucca, Italy. The ancient walls and battlements, still miraculously intact, form the basis of a "belt-park" system which surrounds the city and provides the townsfolk with the only sizable park in the city—albeit narrow in girth and limited in function.

Geneva. Parc Anglais. Europe's park heritage includes elements of the grand and stiffly formal Baroque garden—which fortunately includes the street tree.

Rome. Villa Borghese. This large city park suffers from the inflexibility of a formal past as a grand estate. It suffers more, however, from the intrusion of the automobile.

London.   Sailors on liberty enjoying a respite in the common (J.W. Carmichael, Illustrated London News, 1856).

Los Angeles. Sepulveda Park.   A federal flood control plain, leased by the city and under development as a new park—in the tradition of the English Common (Courtesy Los Angeles City Recreation and Park Department).

London. St. James's Park.   An 1843 drawing of the park, looking North. This view shows the newly completed design by Nash and Repton in the "English Natural" style (Illustrated London News, 1843).

St. James's Park.   Looking west across the lagoon. This park at the very heart of the city, little changed since Nash's time, is the most heavily used park in London.

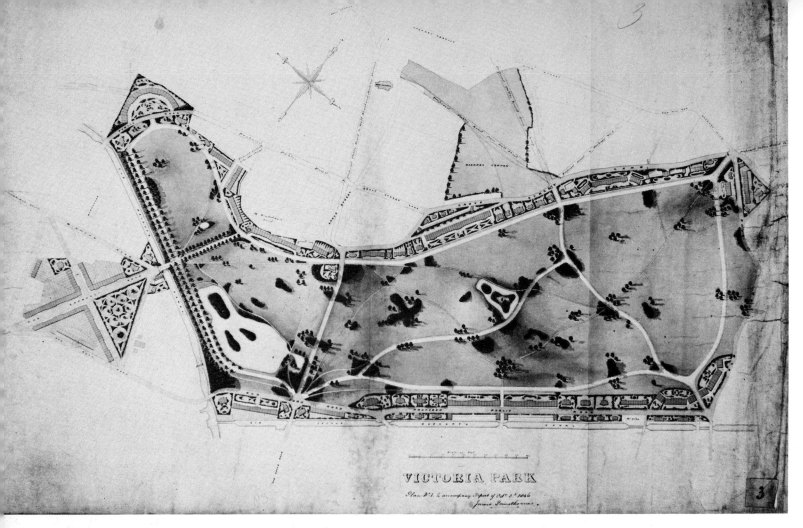

VICTORIA PARK

London. Victoria Park. The first working-class park in the city, located on the East-side where no park or public recreation of any kind had previously existed. This version, dated 1848, is by James Pennethorne, architect for the city of London. It closely follows the 18th Century rules laid down by Lancelot Brown and adapted in the early 19th Century by Repton and Nash (Courtesy Greater London Council).

London. Hampstead Heath. An artist's idealized version of the solution to continuing class problems related to park usage. On this long established common we see all ages and classes apparently coexisting, although at this time (1872) London's Royal Parks were still carefully guarded against intrusion from the working class (Courtesy Illustrated London News).

Nottingham, England. An 1869 drawing of the industrial city, of which Charles Dickens wrote, "the air was blackened and the rivers turned purple." Modern city parks came into existence about this time for the purpose of relieving some of the industrially associated ills. (Courtesy Illustrated London News).

Chicago. Jackson Park.   The "English Natural" introduced to America by Frederick Law Olmsted. Here, on the site of the 1892-1893 World's Columbian Exposition, Olmstead converted the fairgrounds into the graceful aquatic park seen in this aerial photo (Courtesy Chicago Park District).
Below: the perennial gardens in the park reflect the English style.

The "new geometric" park design which emenates from Northern European cities is reflective of the Renaissance gardens of the 16th century, though lacking the rigidity of symmetry and function.
Upper left: A park-square in Stockholm (Courtesy Eric Rosenberg). Lower left: Vondel Park, Amsterdam (Dienst Publicke Werken, Amsterdam). Upper right: Darwin Park, Amsterdam (Dienst Publicke Werken, Amsterdam). Lower right: The "new geometric" adapted to a commercial site in Los Angeles. Often, the hard, forceful lines of a geometric design become an overbearing manipulator of the total concept (Courtesy Aerospace Corp.).

Los Angeles. MacArthur Park. Aerial view of the original "Westlake Park," before World War II. In order to accommodate Westside merchants and financial enterprises, Wilshire Boulevard was extended through the park, making two small parks out of what was once Los Angeles' major natural lake, as seen in lower photograph, taken from the same direction (Courtesy of Harvey Steinberg).

PART 2
THE PARK DEFINED

A SEARCH FOR MEANING

One of the minor tragedies of urban Europe and America has been the failure to develop criteria for modern city parks based on what most city dwellers today would consider to be the social mores of contemporary society. That is to say, the time lag factor and a kind of nostalgia for simpler, more peaceful times have kept park design and especially park development and growth out of step with today's world.

With the exception of Stockholm—and to a lesser degree several other European cities—city park development throughout the western world has failed to keep pace with the dynamic, organic growth and change of their parent cities. The parks have simply remained static or, in many cases, deteriorated in the face of phenomenal urban expansion. The fearsome population explosion is itself a major aspect of urban change; but combined with the multitude of technological advances and social reform, today's rapid growth and development in cities is breathtaking and unprecedented. The rate of urban growth is ever so rapid, because it is expanding in two directions: As the total population of United States increases (130 million in 1940 to 200 million in 1970), the percentage or urban population keeps pace (from 50 percent to nearly 80 percent in the sameperiod).

Consequently our city's parks are too small, too few, poorly located and outdated in terms of design and facilities. Nostalgia has its place, of course. We have museums, historical societies and silent movies. To some extent, the park should continue to pro-vide pleasant memories for a citizenry grown dizzy and weary of rapid change around them. The park offers a little stability to a rootless urban society, jerked about by the scruff from city to city (Americans move every five years according to United States Census reports). Stability is one thing, dessication is another. And the park system, which doesn't grow in step with its parent city, is atrophying, drying up.

Park systems are deteriorating in American cities; because, for one reason, their functions are not completely understood. Their potential, in most instances, has never been fully realized. It is important then to justify the existence of city parks and, in so doing, distinguish between the functions of parks and other public spaces such as squares, malls, school yards and commercial plazas.

The park is distinguished from the square, for example, in being something of a retreat (not escape) from the essential characteristics of urbanism which could be described as exchange, noise, interaction, high density, activity, commerce, etc. The park should not harbor these conditions of city life as does the square nor should it be insulated against them either; because, by so doing, it tends to become an island of escape eschewing all aspects of the city, good and bad. But as an element of contrast, the park offers balance to the urban scene. Such balance is weakened to the extent that purely citified elements are introduced to the park. In our increasingly spectator-oriented society, for instance, the potential value of the park is lessened with the introduction of organized commercial activities, such as professional sports—with their accompanying stadiums—large municipal auditoriums, or highly developed commercial amusement grounds, carnivals, etc. The most essential characteristic of the city park should be self-involvement. The person who enters a park, for whatever purpose and whether alone or accompanied, should bring this involvement with him. The park is serving us best when it offers the framework for enactment of our own productions—be they creative, contemplative, athletic, or merely restful. To the extent that park facilities encourage exploratory and independent activity in a wide range of functions, then to that extent is it answering its primary obligations. Therefore the picnic basket is more reconcilable to the park than the commercially operated restaurant; the restaurant, in turn, becomes more appropriate than the amusement center because of the differences of personal involvement in each.

Can the park then be simply an open space with a few trees while remaining flexible enough for a variety of uses? Definitely, but a good park requires a strong functional organization, good aesthetics, and a sensitive development of scale relationships. Like any successful garden, it requires flexibility for variety of use and a pleasant framework to properly structure those uses. Part of the need is size alone. The necessary contrast with the immediate surroundings and the proper balance with the external forces require sufficient depth. The small park in the urban center is engulfed by its cacophonous and highly charged surroundings. By the very nature of its placid refinement, it can't fight back.

The forces of commercial competition in downtown America are anathema to sound park planning. The very essence of the struggle for private gain dampens a people's response to public well-being and the humanizing of the urban structure in general. Individual effort which is rewarded monetarily leads to individual disinvolvement in terms of urban improvement. Thus the successful Madison Avenue executive drives a fine car, wears expensive clothes, and lives in a beautifully decorated apartment, while walking the filthy streets and breathing polluted air. His expensive apartment overlooks the yellow-green park. From his window, he can observe, through the brown haze, the paper strewn habitation of the defeated, sprawled over the benches and unkempt turf. He sees no strolling lovers, no family picnics under the big oak trees, no bevies of chattering office girls with their bag lunches, or properly attired executives catching a bit of sun while they unfold the Wall Street Journal.

There are, however, animals in the park—large gray rats skulking about the lagoons amongst the refuse—too small to be seen from that far off apartment window. A few row boats splash about guided dispassionately by members of the drop-out society.

Our city parks, like Scrooge's Christmas Eve visions, provide us with a painfully accurate glimpse of the conditions of our civic well-being. The parks, like nothing else in the city, sing the praises of public accomplishment and public trust—the fellowship of man repeated daily. They tell us of public affection and disdain for public institutions as well. Are American cities failing to keep the public trust? Once characterized by such civic criteria as the market square, the cathedral square, the parks and greens, a balanced architectural frame, and a system of avenues and boulevards which synthesized the elements of urbanity into a contiguous whole, the city's most viable aspect of urbanity today appears to be the shopping center. While some of these are remarkable examples of function and beauty—and indications of what we are capable of—their total value to the city is limited. They satisfy only the function of the market square. And even then, they are seldom located organically in respect to the basic growth patterns and related functions of the city, for the rich variety of physical criteria which produce urbanity—cultural, educational, recreational, as well as economical—must remain interrelated. There must be open avenues of civic exchange, even when physical limitations exist. Georges Haussmann in 19th Century Paris, Christopher Wren in 17th Century London, and Sixtus V in 16th Century Rome accomplished such relationships visually where direct physical linkage was not possible.

Isolation, escapism, and compartmentalization of basic urban elements leads to a loss of civic identity and eventual decline of all civic institutions. When economic factors alone prevail, land values, commuter traffic, transportation routes and the like may take dangerous precedence over human factors of growth and development. Thus freeways replace avenues causing greater isolation of parts, resulting in the decaying neighborhood, the lost museum, the hidden zoo, the rundown school, the missing library, the empty auditorium, and the dangerous park. The city park, like other public institutions, is firmly planted in the public trust. What do those two words mean? No amount of federal aid, state and local redevelopment programs, or privately financed urban renewal projects can save our cities if people refuse to accept the meaning—individually and collectively—of those two words.

The city park, with its great promise for recreation, beauty, and balance in our urban environment, is but one criteria of urbanity interlinked with and dependent upon all others. Important government officials and latter-day philosophers tell us that civic strife is primarily caused by unemployment, especially in regards to minorities. But Job Corps, VISTA, and the like are not, by themselves, able to solve the ills of American cities. Realistic answers to difficult and complicated problems are seldom so simple. At some place, we must define the function, meaning, and value of the public park. It is here that civic disorder violently erupted, and it is here that it must be resolved.

On a fine Sunday afternoon, the city's street people gather in large numbers at "Freak Fountain," driving nobody away. On the other side of the nation, a similar group of people attempts to create a park where none existed. Both activities bring on the police, confrontation, and more mistrust—and perhaps, just perhaps, a new beginning.

SYNTHESIS: MEANING INTO FORM

There will be, for most of us, many reasons for liking or disliking a particular park. These can be quite personal—even psychological. There are also many factors of economic, social, and political nature which bear upon the general acceptance and popularity of a park. The degree of urbanity of one city over the next; its weather and topography may impose peculiarities to individual park development. However, there remain only four controllable factors which the landscape architects, planners, and civic officials have any direct opportunity to deal with in creating a successful, enjoyable city park. These are location, shape, size, and design. Each is perhaps equally significant in the proper planning of a city park; but all too often, planning plays little or no part in regard to any of them. For example, location, shape and size are frequently predetermined by a variety of unrelated events long before a particular piece of real estate ever becomes a park.

As in the case of some 17th and 18th Century European estates, many of our modern American city parks had private and very different origins with little bearing on today's park needs. The Wrigley Estate in Pasadena is an example. Built in the early years of the 20th Century, the sumptuous, formal mansion and surrounding grounds have become as difficult as many a Renaissance garden to translate into public park terms. The challenge of Wrigley Park remains unanswered. The Rose Parade Committee uses its facilities seasonally; and for the rest of the year, the park department wonders what to do about picnickers on the front lawn. It is tragic that so few of our American parks have been planned logically in terms of location, shape, and size, as well as the specific relationship needed to support the park system, the public institutions generally, and the immediate surroundings. Inherited parks, like inherited wedding gowns, rarely fit.

Location is usually referred to in regards to park planning from the standpoint of developing of a city-wide system and, as such, is rarely dealt with beyond initial diagram staging. This is unfortunate as satisfactory location of public parks requires much more. Primarily, criteria must be established to determine a city's park needs. These cannot be arbitrary or haphazard but must result from an honest evaluation of public opinion. Then ratios must be developed, such as proper distance between parks, optimum persons per park acre, time and distance limits for traveling to nearest park, proper balance of facilities provided, and so on. Such should be the proper responsibilities of the park commission rather than the city employee, as it is the commissioners, elected or appointed, who represent the residents and, therefore, carry the obligation of setting standards and criteria. It will fall to the park department and city officials generally to carry these out.

Such criteria, when sharpened by the various limitations imposed by reality, will become the basis for location of new parks and the restructuring of old. In the case of established areas, residential or not, it is important that long range plans for park land acquisition be made in view of the shifting dynamic quality of

42

urban growth patterns. New residential developments—for example, high-rise complexes built to replace low income slum housing—badly need accompanying park sites where originally there may have been neither the need nor the opportunity. Contrary to popular planning creed, commercial and even industrial property may sometimes revert to residential use. In Pomona, California, a large manufacturer of heavy equipment recently abandoned its centrally-located 40-acre plant, leaving the city with a golden opportunity for centralized redevelopment. Usually such shifts in the fortunes of big business and industry can be spotted well ahead and planned for accordingly. Therefore, a master park plan should be developed by the park commission and, along with the established criteria governing its structure, should remain flexible and relevant to the city's overall master plan, thus permitting the park commission to be in a position to take positive action when opportunities arise.

Finally, a park's location means quite a lot to its immediate surroundings. Whether they be commercial, residential, or a mixture of both, the city can expect a general increase in land values, a decrease in vacancies, and an improvement in appearance following development of adjacent park land. In view of vandalism, loss of tax revenues, and increased fire and police protection, the location of a new park can be a very real asset to the neighborhood and to the city as well.

Size, like location, can best be determined by the implementation of developed criteria—of needs vs. budget, but a park's size is rarely predetermined in this way. Even when land has been originally set aside for park development, the size and location are often merely the result of decisions made by the subdivider—a sop to the city council and planning commission—and may not reflect even remotely the various established criteria.

Often topographic limitations to development determine size and location of city parks. A meandering and sometimes unpredictable stream, an arroyo, an open drainage channel, a severe change in grade, or a poorly drained low spot may lend themselves to park development by reason of being unsuited to other kinds of development. In such cases, criteria for park planning, reasonably flexible of course, need to be studied. Parks must be located where they can best serve the city's needs—in accordance with a planned system rather than as a result of expedience or caprice. On the other hand, natural as well as man-made phenomena within the city should be studied for their potential value towards incorporation into parks. The boggy areas around London were set aside to remain in their natural state, largely because of drainage problems. They became, unofficially, the first parks of London; and today gigantic Wimbledon Common, in its glorious wilderness, is invaluable to the well-being of that sprawling metropolis. In Southern California, the many drainage channels and settling basins could be developed into channel or ribbon parks allowing frequent nodal points for intensified activities. Two large basins, created by flood control dams, have become city parks in Los Angeles. In a similar way, that city's freeway system, with its ample green borders, produces a network of lineal visual parks. With the introduction of nodal collection points reached from the freeway or otherwise, these visual parks could be projected into an interlocking lineal park system, unique to this sprawling, motorized city but all-encompassing in its breadth potential. Such a park system could be effective in reestablishing the linkage between adjacent parts which the freeways have severed. Water towers, located always on high points and on public land, can become giant size park sculpture, or double as observation towers and even restaurants. In the case of dwindling river trade, the old commercial water front docks can give way to new river front parks, giving the local populace an opportunity to discover anew the beauty and heritage of their river front settlement. And in view of the shifting fortunes of commerce, due to changes in transportation, the recreational and tourist trade may well prove monetarily more successful.

In Claremont, California, an unused commercial strip along a railroad right-of-way separated from adjacent housing by a 30-foot embankment, apparently had little to offer as a potential neighborhood park site. But its central location was a positive factor; and it is being developed as a special-use park for organized sports—mainly, league baseball and football for youngsters. This, in turn, will greatly reduce the pressure of these activities on the various neighborhood parks of the city where informal, pick-up games are more in order.

It should be noted, however, that in determining park size by use of established criteria, there is more than projected function involved, in terms of a park's potential uses. Size alone is a significant factor in the determination of the site's value. One ten-acre park site has more potential in terms of facilities, variety, and importance to the city than do two five-acre sites. A pie, for example, which will serve four persons adequately should not be stretched to twelve slices, as no one in this instance will have had any real satisfaction from having had dessert. Likewise, postage stamp parks, which are to small to offer more than limited recreational possibilities and moreover provide little or no refuge from their noisy surroundings, would serve better if combined into a

single park of respectable size. Some might have to walk a few blocks further; but for park (or pie) of sufficient proportions, it should be worth it.

But what represents sufficient *size*? That again needs to be determined by criteria, ratios, and goals, of course. But in doing so, one might consider the variety of activities, the opportunities for experience, the magnitude, the civic pride and sheer greatness of Paris' *Bois de Boulogne* (3,000 acres), Amsterdam's *Amsterdamse Bos* (2,500 acres), or Philadelphia's Fairmount Park (4,000 acres). Only large parks can offer the great variety of active and passive recreational pursuits (including city-wide to international attractions) as well as the sublime vastness of wooded retreat. St. Louis' Forest Park, partly the residual of the 1904 World's Fair, contains the internationally acclaimed Muni Opera and the nation's leading zoological gardens. Golden Gate Park in San Francisco attracts the world's visitors to its Japanese Gardens, Art Museum, horticultural displays and aquarium. (Unfortunately, it also maintains more than its share of nonconforming facilities and high speed thoroughfares.) Central Park in New York, one of the smallest of the world's major city parks, houses few such attractions but remains the most significant and valuable piece of open space in that city. Its size and location have given hard-pressed New Yorkers recreation and retreat for a hundred years.

Size can and should be determined. Minimum size of a neighborhood park should be based on the number of persons to be served, their basic social patterns, and the direction and distance to the next park. A great city park, serving not only its immediate surroundings but the entire city and even a considerable tourist trade as well, cannot be so easily assessed in terms of size. But it is easy to see how favorably Fairmount Park compares with Central Park by sheer force of size. The external pressure exerted on the latter, an effect produced mainly by its grid shape and limited size, helps to establish its character as an escape park, while much larger Fairmount Park engenders its own pressure from within and tends to force its image onto the city. Consequently, Philadelphia is physically affected and, to some extent, shaped by this park which is almost a system within itself, while Central Park, on the other hand, is continually faced by external threat. Since the basic characteristic of the city park is its compliant, feminine nature, size is perhaps her greatest hope of withstanding rape and intimidation by aggressive, competitive surroundings.

The next important factor in city park development is *shape*. Normally rectangular, as derived from the conventional grid system of American street patterns, the average city park could be greatly improved if its shape could be adjusted to better meet local conditions and neighborhood needs. The rectangular shape does not result from any attempt to improve neighborhood conditions but rather from expedience in plotting and apparently a lack of understanding on the part of the original developer. Encroaching streets can be removed later; but, for the most part, a park's general character—its limitations and relationship to its surroundings—are made with the original layout of streets and underground facilities. For this reason, it is imperative that park design commence with the initial development of any new area. Thus advance planning may locate a park site and also determine its size well ahead of design and development. Established park system criteria require that such progressive planning be accomplished so as to safeguard the system in the future. A little thought towards more imaginative park shaping as well can produce:

a. Greater integration with the surrounding neighborhood,
b. Greater safety and protection against excessive through traffic adjacent to the park,
c. Better potential organization for internal park design,
d. Transitional areas or "lead in" strips for better pedestrian access to the park,
e. Visual connectors to create greater continuity between parks, traffic systems, and civic facilities generally, and
f. More flexibility in achieving aesthetic and practical use of natural topographic features.

The following examples are neighborhood park prototypes, illustrating variations in form and arrangement within the limitations imposed by the gridiron street system of most American cities:

In illustration (A) the gridiron-formed park encompassing four blocks is all but predesigned by external conditions. In this configuration the park faces the minimum number of blocks (eight), is subject to the maximum adjacent traffic, but offers the greatest depth—*i.e.*, escape from surrounding audio and visual encroachment, and an increase in internal flexibility. Illustration (B) exposes the park to greater neighborhood contact. It faces ten blocks. The advantage in aesthetic contact is paid for by a diminished depth and consequent decrease in flexibility potential. It also suffers from maximum adjacent through traffic.

Illustration (C) is a compromise solution. It faces eight blocks but two have a double exposure, equalling that of illustration (B). The depth and flexibility of (A) are retained however, with the added advantage of a configuration more conducive to the accommodation of variable park functions, as: central open space for active field play, and areas at either end for specific development (tot-lot, community building, courts, passive areas). The end areas serve as connectors to the surrounding neighborhood and separators (protectors) of the central space, which is the focus or heart of the park.

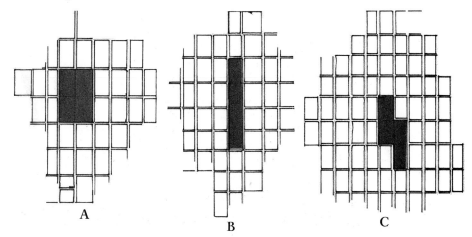

A B C

In illustration (D) pedestrian lead-ins are included for the purpose of providing a more intensified linkage with the neighborhood. These "green walks," here arranged in a pin-wheel plan, greatly increase a sense of integration between park and home without appreciably increasing the park's size. Heavy through traffic adjacent to the park is also discouraged. Illustration (E) employs four small parks, arranged in pin-wheel relationship, in an effort towards larger urban organization, by which the system of linking parks separates and coordinates neighborhoods. Such a system can be used to reduce the seemingly endless, amorphous sprawl of residential development in low density cities, and provide a sense of individuality and scale to each green belted complex.

The larger, centrally located city park (illustration F), arranged in simple rectangular form, may suffer further separation from its surroundings by being bounded on all four sides by heavy trafficked thoroughfares. Such avenues, located by city planners and traffic commissioners for aesthetic convenience tend to create an insular quality in the park, making it more difficult to reach by foot. The advantage is all to the passerby, following the same line of reasoning which locates highways and rail-lines along beaches, parks and lakefronts. The park users are the losers. The same park could have been protected against separation and exposure by adjusting its configuration at the outset, as shown in illustration (G). Insulation against traffic and better neighborhood contact are both thereby accomplished. In illustration (H) a further advantage of the pin-wheel design is apparent. Here is seen the emergence of neighborhood identification, created by major thoroughfares and the park on each of two sides. In combination with other parks of similar design, and planned as a total system along with coordination of traffic, neighborhood groupings, commercial areas and urban character generally can be physically determined by means of internal green belts. As communities develop and adjust inwardly as well as toward the surrounding parks, the sense of identity, individuality and communal association can be expected to deepen.

Finally, in regard to topography, it can be seen that by allowing natural configuration of the landscape to dictate boundaries, greater park integrity can be more successfully achieved. This is not to suggest that city parks in general should be made to resemble nature in the same manner as has been attempted in the past. Nostalgia for "poetic naturalism" may no longer be practical or even realistic under modern urban conditions, but strong physical features of the land should be recognized in both vertical and lateral dimensions. Thus a natural waterway, a sharp change in elevation, a stand of native trees, can be treated naturally in recog-

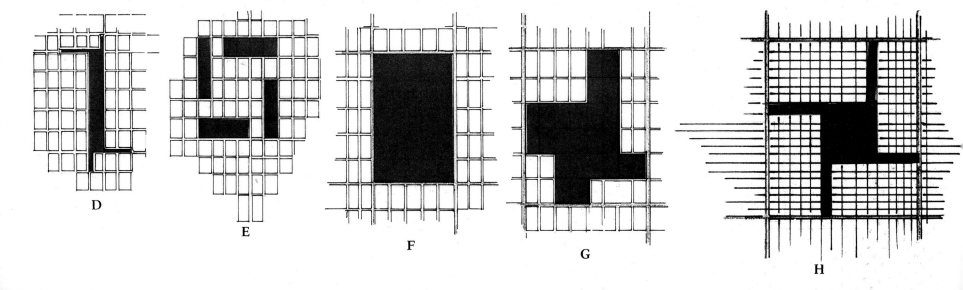

D

E

F

G

H

nition of intrinsic, organic beauty. It may also be possible, and sometimes more applicable, to solve problems of awkward topography with fresh, new urbanistic concepts. The methods by which vertical and lateral shaping are produced can be originative and aesthetic. For example, natural streamways or drainage channels need not become box-walled open sewers with accompanying offensive chain-link fences for protection. Where naturalized solutions are not possible due to high density, erosion, and flooding dangers, new architectonic solutions are needed which retain the original beauty while couching it in urbanistic terms. The San Antonio River Park (San Antonio, Texas) is an early example of such design awareness. Always a flood threat, the San Antonio River snaked through the city in a great ox-bow form which was eventually rounded out and stabilized during the depression years under the auspices of the Works Progress Administration. Today it ranks with the Alamo as the city's finest attraction, and as a park is far superior. In *Parc Buttes–Chaumont,* Paris the artificial topography created by abandoned slag piles and quaries was intensified by the park designer in order to create spectacular effects.

Thus location, size, and shape are important factors in the ultimate success of individual parks and total park systems and cannot be allowed to revert to developers or even urban planners without the input of those responsible to the people for the proper implementation of its park system. Then the proper design of parks can follow.

FUNCTIONS AND PRIORITIES: PREREQUISITES TO DESIGN

The most significant aspect of the four controllable factors in park development should be the design itself—the internal manipulation of circulation, spaces, and facilities, in proper balance, in order to achieve in the most efficient and aesthetic manner goals previously established. And what are those objectives?

Before the design is attempted and throughout the various stages toward completion, the responsible parties should be aware of three stages of development in park design. The first of these is purpose—the goals, broadly stated and flexibly interpreted, which hopefully will be realized in the final design. If an overriding philosophy exists on the part of the parks commission, the council, and the working department then purpose can readily be translated into concrete terms—what the park or park system is expected to provide.

In the beginning, we differentiated in terms of purpose between the park and the square. While the Athenian Agora provided aspects of both, the more structured societies that followed narrowed the capabilities of urban space somewhat, while emphasizing the masculine characteristics of urbanism—noise, activity, exchange, competition (including masculine symbolism in the form of some dominant vertical shaft or sculpture), while de-emphasizing the feminine—contemplation, relaxation, solitude. To be of value in the highly charged and wearying urban environment, the city park must provide these latter needs. Therefore it remains for the park to provide urban balance in an otherwise overcharged, commercial atmosphere.

Such a distinction between the differing needs and philosophies of public open space—park and square—has been woefully lacking in contemporary interpretation, resulting in the misuse and confusion of purpose concerning the two.

The second stage of design development involves the determination of park functions. Based on a philosophy of purpose, such functions should relate to the broadest possible concepts of endeavor. Eventually such functions can be translated into specific facilities, interruption of priorities, and loss of total scope of the park project. Too often, the new park site will be subject to finite decisions prior to any program of purpose and function. ("Let's put a cannon there in the middle." "I know where we can get an old fire engine cheap." "Kids like baseball." "Shouldn't we have a tennis court?") Functions should reflect the people's needs, and these will vary considerably from a neighborhood park of 20 acres to a 1000-acre downtown park meant to serve all the city. The park can be a bridge to better communication within the city which is so badly needed at this time. The functions of a park must then be vital to this endeavor. Such functions have to do with experiencing. Experience yourself. Experience others. Communicate.

How is this done? In many ways, both passive and active. By walking, for one. A fair-sized city park can provide a tremendous assortment of experiences to the stroller—a variety of things to see, the feel of different materials under foot, odors, sounds, and the pleasant sensations of physical exertion. Park paths designed for the pleasure of walking, and not merely for the purpose of reaching some destination may successfully offer all of these and more.

In Parc Bagatelle (Paris) essentially little beyond the simple pleasure of strolling is offered, but in such a pleasant way as to constantly afford visitors a variety of interests and surprises, such as the artificial grottoes, water features, and the continually changing floral plantings. Amsterdam's giant Amsterdamse Bos provides seemingly endless paths leading into a wonderland of exploration—and all carefully separated from vehicular ways—through dark and dripping primeval forests, out again into sunny glades, along gentle canals and wide lagoons. When one tires of walking in this great wilderness park, he can drift awhile along the grass-banked canals.

Or resting. The park is a place to sit or lie down on a fine day. Feel the sun on your face on a chilly day or the cool breezes on a warm one. Feel all the elements about you. Feel the grass with your toes. Notice how the earth yields under you—as paved surfaces never do. In Northern European cities, a warm and sunny spring day has a remarkable effect on people. In secluded glens at Kew Gardens, London shop girls change into bikinis in order to capture those long-awaited rays. In Copenhagen or Stockholm, people will strip off as much clothing as they can for a half hour's respite at noon in a sun-filled pocket of a downtown park.

Such a place within the city, such a park, gives us the chance to investigate not only natural surroundings but ourselves as well. Here one can ponder life's destiny, or plan a coming event, or read a book. Alone. There is something rather frightening in our society today which works to prevent solitude, and yet the benefits of such self-indulgence as quiet contemplation should be obvious.

Here is a place to reflect; come to grips with oneself over the day's activities or life itself. Kids can make new friends. A man sits with his wife over a picnic and rediscovers things about her he had all but forgotten. A group of young people sit in a circle with a couple of guitars. Do they sing about the beauty of life or protest its inequities? Some may practice things which parts of our society do not condone; but it should be noted that such behavior is characteristic of the time, not the parks. Remember, activities which take place in the park reflect conditions which exist outside its boundaries. Cities may suggest closing parks to prevent drug trafficking and the like, just as many parks were closed in the late 40's and early 50's to prevent integration. In the name of protection, city parks have often been emasculated—robbed of their beauty and excitement by being reduced to flat green platforms with trees pruned to permit the searching eye of authority.

In view of our fears and restrictions in park usage the following letter from a French woman to Jack Smith (of the *Los Angeles Times*) seems strangely poignant and nostalgic:

"Right in the midst of my home town" (wrote Michele Mooney), "in the Province of Lorraine, in France, there is an esplanade; a park fashioned after Versailles. It is a public park. There is a fountain, a music kiosk, benches, chairs, flower beds, balloon vendors, a pool for the children's toy sailing boats, groves for lovers . . . just a park.

"Beside grannies pushing prams, there are college students reciting theses to one another; little boys in shorts blowing in the sails of their vessels on the edge of the pool; and many times, so many times, a distraught child sees his ship beyond reach, and a nice man can be espied silently removing laced shoes and knee-high socks to wade in the miniature lake in pursuit of the toy boat.

"In the esplanade" (continues Ms. Mooney), "one meets 'hard hats' having lunch while reading the daily paper; some dozing transients; knitting aunts, and old knightly-mannered gentlemen with molehair hats and buttoned spats.

"And young mothers; and new mothers perhaps not as young. And all are real . . . Mothers so proud when a gentleman doffs his hat to them and smiles at the cuddled bundles of pink or blue held tight; winters and summers, on the benches of the esplanade, mothers nurse their babies with pride; with that basic nobility which endows women in love."

Such a tranquil blending of people and events reminds us again of the need for genuine trust and respect at all levels of social order—without which the park cannot succeed as an urban institution.

Children still go to the park to play. Men go to gymnasiums, but their purposes are the same. We delight in our bodies, what they can do. We delight in the pleasures they bring us—a game of catch, a chinning bar, a pick-up softball game. Thus, the park allows people to find out something about themselves and others through playing, talking, singing, eating. Such are the functions of the city park.

Learning is also a park function. All kinds of educational programs, not otherwise obtainable, are possible here. In addition to many recreational pursuits, we can have such things as music and drama workshops for all ages. There are learning experiences connected with organized sports as well.

And, of course, there is the zoo. But the best instructional experience to be gained in the park, however, comes from its natural base. It gives a nature-starved urban population some contact with its roots. Certainly a city park is not expected to duplicate nature, and those romanticized visions of the 19th Century may not be altogether valid today; but neither can a metropolis of several million people be expected to embrace nature by means of a row of carefully spaced and shaped street trees, projecting identically from their geometric bases, or from indoor tropicals and potted window boxes of geraniums, colorful and agreeable as they might be. Such examples represent nature's yielding to urbanistic demands. They are architectonic solutions; and they pervade the square, the campus, and the park as well. The danger here lies in the potential loss in balance between town and park. This danger becomes a reality when a basic purpose of the park—*contrast*—is

lost or forgotten. The *"New Geometric,"* in its haste to eliminate nostalgic and sometimes inefficient uses—swans, rustic bridges, theatrical effects—threatens to reduce that contrast between town and park to minimal levels. Hopefully park personnel will acknowledge that regardless of changing demands of modern living, natural patterns and habits of life remain, including contact with organic roots.

The third stage in park development is the final physical design including the development of facilities. For example, walking, the function, leads to the creation of paths. Eating may lead to a picnic (first priority) or restaurant (second priority, because commercial interests belong more to the square than the park). Playing means open fields, backstops, courts and various kinds of equipment but not stadiums, arenas, or sports palaces of any kind. (Spectator sports, commercialism and their accompanying sedentary crowds have no place in the public park.) Climbing and swinging suggest various kinds of equipment, some of which have resulted in bizarre and beautiful forms, the test of which must always be their ability to challenge and delight children. Play equipment, which offers little opportunity for a child to investigate and conquer, whether expensive fiberglass creations or junked war planes, has little purpose in the master plan of park design. It is indeed folly to permit service clubs and other local help-meets to engage directly in the development of park design. Fire engines, jet planes, rockets, and the like stand today in mute testimony to capricious planning.

Child psychologists, school teachers, naturalists, and recreation leaders are much more likely consultants to the park designer. It is probably a mistake, we are told, to provide a park with too many facilities which are fixed or predetermined as to use, especially if intended for children's use. Child psychologists tell us that young minds require more generalized forms of play equipment in order that their active imaginations can be called into play to fill in the details. Except for specific activities such as tennis, shuffleboard, and the like, the same approach to active recreation can be applied to adults as well. Imagination, exploration, unstructured awareness offer the base for development of park space and facilities most likely to remain viable through the years.

A basic outline for city park development should then be:

1. Location
2. Size
3. Shape
4. Design
   a. purpose
   b. function
   c. form

With this in mind, we are free to examine three areas of more specific function which have usually maintained high priorities in our major city parks.

Sports, a prime consideration in park planning, can be separated from general active play by distribution of organizational requisites, the fewer of which are needed, the better. Thus in regard to sports activities, a distinct priority of athletic activity should be arranged, keeping in mind that less structured and more participatory games are the most desirable. A priority check list for baseball might show the following:

1. Pick-up softball, no schedules, no equipment provided;
2. Sand lot or little league with scheduling called for;
3. Semi-pro municipal leagues, with night lighting and bleachers; and
4. Professional league, with stadium parking lot, ticket booths, and traffic jams.

The first and second priority listings might be all that any large park could tolerate. Certainly number four should be dropped from any kind of priority list. We need not look far to find examples which clearly indicate the detrimental effect on parks brought about by the intrusion of commercial sports palaces. Kezar Stadium has had a deleterious effect on Golden Gate Park's east end—no doubt worse than Haight-Asbury. Dodger Stadium has crippled Elysian Park, and nearby Exposition Park serves only as a somewhat pleasant entrance to Los Angeles' Coloseum. Spectator palaces, stadiums, and arenas, like the great amphitheaters of ancient Rome, are primarily intended as commercial entertainment. They provide no opportunity for self-involvement, physical or mental. They operate on schedules, attracting large crowds, necessitating huge parking lots. Their fans have little or no interest in adjacent park activities and are likely to cause them inconvenience or even damage. Additional vehicular access is required, producing congestion, noise and danger. Pedestrian scope is shortened, open space reduced, tranquility shattered. Although the 49'ers have departed in search of grayer pastures (more available parking) the problem of nonconforming usage will remain as long as Kezar Stadium stands.

Why do city governments permit the building of sports palaces in parks? Because the land is there. Nothing need be torn down but trees, and they are inexpensive to remove. "It's kind of pleasant, and there's lots of space for parking," goes the argument. But especially, there is all that revenue, in the form of taxes, for the city. Parks cost money; and cities in this wealthiest of nations in history are, in the words of Boston's Mayor, Kevin White, "on the verge of bankruptcy." There are some paying propositions open to the destitute park commissions which are less drastic. Golf courses occupy much of the developed acreage in Griffith Park (Los Angeles) and Forest Park (St. Louis). While golf avoids fixed schedules, spectator crowds, parking lots, noise and congestion, it is, however, not ideal as a park facility in that it requires committing large acreage to low density, single purpose use. Griffith Park's five courses consume about 75 percent of the total developed acreage while serving only a small percentage of the park's users. As for the profit incentive, while it is true that park facilities which pay their own way or even return a profit to the city are favored by many a councilman and taxpayer, this should not become a major consideration in park planning. The charging of fees in a park, no matter the benefactor, tends to take away from a major role of the park—that of providing retreat from business, trade, and commercial activities in general. Before any fee-charging programs are planned, a careful evaluation of their possible effects on the park should be made. For certain facilities or programs which the budget cannot adequately manage, fees may be inevitable. Bowling greens, shuffleboard, or bocce courts may be developed by retired citizens in cooperation with the park department and maintained jointly.

Other such limited interest programs may be expected to receive some private support. Classes in art, music, dancing, and swimming may require fees to pay for instruction. Water skiing, boating, and the like may draw a permit charge to defray costs. All such charges are considered legitimate if their operating expenses tend to bring an undue burden on the city—or the taxpayers who, by and large, do not take advantage of such programs. Fee charging, however, can easily get out of hand. An overdose of charges tends to remove the park and its facilities from the public domain. The citizen can't be expected to believe it's his park if he has to pay for everything he uses.

Theatre in the park is another important activity suggesting careful study. Such large, open air productions as the Greek Theatre in Griffith Park and the Muni Opera in Forest Park have city-wide if not international reputations. They provide a variety of professional entertainment at all prices—there are cheap, grass seats and free areas at the Muni—bringing civic pride to the parent cities as well as to the parks. They also represent nonconforming use for the park in that they operate on fixed schedules, are basically spectator oriented, occupy large areas not usable for any other purpose, and subject the park to major traffic intrusion. In spite of such limitations, large, outdoor professional theatres should be adapted to city park systems where their inclusion will not seriously damage a park's plan or major value to the city. This takes size. Griffith Park (4,000 acres) can easily handle the intrusion, while the Hollywood Bowl, managed by Los Angeles County Park Department, remains a park with a singular function. More in keeping with the noncommercial, nonspectator orientation of public parks are the many theatre workshops, puppet and marionette-

making classes and drama clubs which can operate from the park. In this category can be found the local band concert, dance festivals, group songfests, and home-grown carnivals. In California and New York in particular, a veritable renaissance of production arts is taking place, involving school kids, teachers, parents and neighborhoods in general. Park departments can encourage participatory park theatrics and festivals by providing good, flexible facilities and some professional instruction. Collapsible stages are inexpensive and disappear when not in use, allowing for a greater degree of efficiency in overall park planning. The local high school can be tapped for talent such as drama, dance, and music teachers as well as coaches and art teachers.

During the last few years, American parks have witnessed the love-in, a unique and truly American phenomenon through which people of all ages have experienced a revival of genuine mutual respect and cooperation—something which had all but disappeared within the bubble syndrome of private cars, television, and single family detached dwellings. Such amateur theatre and do-it-yourself entertainment ought to be continually encouraged by park commissions as logical and healthy functions of the city park. Towards this end, Mayor White himself has emerged as a prominent figure in the Boston Park Deparment's recent experiments in street theatre and related programs in neighborhood self-involvement. Mayor White and his forward thinking park staff may be a vanguard of a renaissance in city park programming. And the amazing thing is that much of their efforts to date do not even require the facilities of the park as such. It is, at least in spirit, the beginnings of a park movement such as found in Stockholm, where theatre programs and recreational programs emanating from the park take hold of an entire community. All of our park departments should be encouraged to promote such programming in the neighborhood or community which is considered to be appropriate and necessary—regardless of availability of funds and facilities. And keeping in touch with community leaders is vital in this pursuit. In 1970 community response to developmental plans for an East Los Angeles neighborhood park was immediate, strong and volatile. As a result, local leaders of this primarily Mexican American neighborhood have brought about a complete redesign along desired cultural lines. At the same time in Claremont, California, park personnel stayed in touch with the community's youth and planned two summer night street dances. Both were highly successful and went far towards cementing better relations between young people and the local business community, who cooperated with the park department in this endeavor. In Boston, Claremont and many American cities, Park Administration personnel are beginning to listen to the people. It's a hopeful sign. Art, in various forms and levels of quality, owns a place in the park. Sculpture plays a prominent and traditional role, reflecting the social and political character of the surrounding culture—from stern bronze horsemen to carefree wood nymphs.

But sculpture in the park need not be limited to the noble (and costly) works of the anointed few. Presumptuous councils and civic groups have on occasion persuaded college and high school art students (and faculty) to donate their time and talents towards the creation of park sculpture—nonobjective works out of driftwood, great wind driven stabiles made from scrap metal, and short-term pieces from cloth and paper. Carl Milles, the great Swedish sculptor, set the tone for park sculpture in his native land and today Stockholm's parks, and most Swedish cities, are filled with the whimsical, delightful prancing forms by Milles and his followers.

Displays of paintings, protected against the weather, or works by students which have no great value beyond their immediate aspect, are striking in contrast with the park's soft greens. The experiments in neighborhood painting, successfully carried out by the Watts Workshop in Los Angeles, and other similar artistic endeavors by local talents, suggests the feasibility of experimental art work in the parks. City Councils should encourage any variety of imaginative programs to enliven the parks through ongoing projects in the visual arts.

Somewhere within a major city's park system will be found a zoo. Originally labeled "zoological garden," the city zoo in the United States ranks amongst public achievements anywhere between "pride of the state" to "a civic disgrace." Often it has been the ingenuity and foresight of one man, such as George Vierheller or Marlin Perkins, which has been responsible for establishing the concept of permanent enclosures of exotic creatures for the amusement and edification of local citizens. Historically a by-product of the carnival and traveling circus, the concept of a "zoological garden" was incorporated into the theme of the 1904 St. Louis World's Fair by a creative genius, David R. Francis. Thus wild creatures from all over the world were brought to Missouri and housed in naturalized compounds made up largely of red granite boulders rather than the tacky cages of traveling circuses or lesser zoos. Here in realistic surroundings, the ferocious beasts of distant continents thrilled fair-goers and established the "zoological garden" as a fixed institution in St. Louis. Most of the buildings and exhibits were removed at the fair's end; but the zoo remained, and has, over the years, increased in size and scope, becoming the standard by which all other zoos are measured.

In addition, Forest Park, a gently rolling site of 1,200 acres on the city's western edge, most of which had been used for the fair, was retained as a city park. Thus park and zoo became firmly associated with one another in St. Louis—a relationship so natural as to be adhered to almost without exception wherever major zoos are found.

In planning the future urban parks, the status of the zoo must therefore be investigated; and in an attempt to do so, certain questions should be raised, as:

1. Are zoos any longer necessary?
2. Do zoos really belong in the city park?

According to Desmond Morris, the noted zoologist, the heyday of the zoological garden is over. Its earlier popularity depended largely on the naive curiosity of those recent arrivals to the cities—the masses of rural folk who left the farms to seek a better life in the rapidly expanding industrial might of the great cities.

Today's more sophisticated urbanites have less fascination for caged wild animals, partly because of mass communication advances. As Morris sees it, movies and television have brought us into close contact with beasts of the wild, so much so that firsthand experience with caged and forlorn specimens often pales by comparison.

The future of such a traditional zoological garden thus appears limited, even as cities continue to plan for them. Morris suggests that the hope for zoos in Europe, as well as in America, lies in the search for new and meaningful avenues of use, not just innovation but as a result of serious re-evaluation of the purpose of animal display. For zoos to succeed in the future, more than mere observation is going to be necessary. That was all right when nobody had ever seen a bear; but on that basis alone, only the very young will remain good customers. In St. Louis the zoo's continuing successes have always resulted from growth and change. The first national zoo to remove bars began, in the 1930's, to feature circus performances including individual scheduled shows with lions, chimpanzees, and elephants. Other innovations followed. On a warm Sunday afternoon, visitors strolling on the zoo's garden paths might be startled by a sudden honk from behind to discover an impatient motorized chimp driving about his domain in a miniature electric run-about.

In San Diego innovation and new concepts in animal display have also been successful. Beautiful Balboa Park, site of the 1915 Panama Exposition and later the 1935 California Pacific Exposition, follows the history of St. Louis' Forest Park—first, a great fairground which was later to become the city's major public park. And today each of these great parks houses world famous zoos, noted for their popular inventiveness. The children's zoo, walk-through bird enclosures and the rugged natural setting are amongst the San Diego Zoo's major attractions. Near Los Angeles a recent private venture in zoological innovation was opened. Lion Country Safari is almost directly copied from Kruger National Park in South Africa, featuring a drive (in your own car) through a lion infested landscape. Not to be outdone the City of San Diego more recently opened its vast new "Wild Animal Park" a few miles northeast of the city on a rolling, arid landscape not unlike the African steppe. Instead of lions the new park offers a near ecological balance in African wildlife—exclusive of predators. The San Diego experiment makes a singular contribution to wild animal parks which even Kruger and the other African parks may someday come to emulate. In place of private automobiles visitors are transported through the grounds by electric tram.

While circus acts, children's zoos, naturalized enclosures and such have proved to be successful, Morris and others believe much more will be necessary in the future to assure the zoological garden a major place in our cities and parks. American cities are increasing rapidly in population and perhaps more significantly in percentage of the total population. As metropolitan sprawl continues to gobble up surrounding rural and natural areas, fewer Americans each year remain on the farms and in the small towns of the countryside. Los Angeles occupies almost 500 square miles of urbanized landscape; and its surrounding metropolitan area, including some sixty contiguous incorporated cities, covers much more. Today school children from Harlem and other densely inhabited sections of New York are bussed to Central Park—in order to discover grass! In the near future, the major American city parks, if they are allowed to remain, will increasingly be expected to perform this function. And the more natural they remain, the more successful they will be in helping poverty kids to understand nature, ecology, and the basic life forces underlying even the most urbanized society.

Some psychologists, as well as Desmond Morris, believe the zoo has a new role to play in teaching city folk about their natural heritage. For example, the domestic zoo, with its goats, chickens and milking cows, may hold more meaning for a ghetto child than caged lions and tigers. Moreover a native zoo combining animals and plants of the local region may give a child a better understanding of natural selection and ecological order—something our forefathers took for granted. Ingenious enclosures could be devised which would allow for study and observation without restricting the animal's natural habitat. Native animal sanctuaries might require a minimal effort on the visitor's part in order to catch sight of the inhabitants; but as anyone who has spotted a deer or bear in one of our national parks will attest, that is precisely what makes it worthwhile.

One of the oldest native animal zoos in the country, The Desert Museum, near Tucson is presently expanding its facilities for holding and displaying its collection of regional desert creatures. The new enclosures are ingeniously devised to reflect the rugged terrain while offering maximum visibility to visitors and freedom to animals (overly so for the Desert Bighorn sheep who bolted their enclosure after being there but three minutes). William Conway, curator of the Bronx Zoo in New York, calls the Desert Museum the best of its kind and a forerunner to future zoological planning.

Following the free and natural antics of a nearby squirrel is often more interesting than watching the repetitious and pathetic pacing of a caged leopard. In fact the large city park will usually manage to harbor a good number of four-legged escapees from the city's noise and congestion, making it a natural zoo of sorts anyway. Obviously some innovative animal displays are beyond the possibility of conventional zoos. There remains a considerable difference in concept and purpose between a circus ring and an ecological enclosure. Park zoos cannot be both, to any degree of depth; but insofar as a sense of identity between urban populace and wildlife can be developed, the large city park probably by itself remains the basis of commonality for such an endeavor. If for some park visitors the squirrels, sparrows, and pigeons represent a more meaningful relationship between urban man and nature, then all the better.

Today's large, centrally located city parks will normally provide most of the really unique facilities inherent to park development as well as for the parent city itself. The danger of this practice lies in the making of a storehouse out of the park by including, within its bounds, every manner of nonconforming function or facility which civic-minded individuals over the years can dream up. At the neighborhood level, this might include war memorials, rose arbors, service club facilities and all manner of projects accomplished with private funds and perhaps intended for restricted use. At a larger scale, the list of nonconforming uses can become enormous, including hospitals, police target ranges, reservoirs and power plants. San Francisco's Golden Gate Park is an example. Because of its beauty, size, and location, various groups have, for over a century, managed to obtain permission to locate facilities of narrow interest in the park. The neighborhood park, which is unattached to a public school, has a need for some community facilities—meeting hall, clubrooms, and such. The large park would be better off in most cases without them, or at least they should be kept near the perimeters. Besides community halls and academies, the rule of perimeter location needs to be applied to museums, libraries, auditoriums, commercial stadiums and arenas, theatres, and all such civic structures and facilities with primarily a singular function and a limited relationship to the park as a whole. When located well inside the boundaries of the park, such facilities bring people into the park but not to use it as primarily intended. This results in more roads, vehicular congestion, noise, and parking problems. When a park-located facility attracts large crowds on fixed schedules, the problems may become acute, as in the case of commercial sports.

There are, of course, different circumstances surrounding the planning of facilities for neighborhood as well as city-wide parks. Certain of these belong in every community park, such as fixed play equipment, passive gathering areas and open space for active play. Certain other activities or facilities may have unique or one-to-a-city character, and thereby should be situated in a city-wide park. For a town of 10,000 people, such unique features might include the public swimming pool and tennis courts, while a great metropolis might feature the zoo, amphitheatre, a sailing lagoon, and horse trails. No matter the variation in size, this differentiation between neighborhood facilities and city-wide park facilities must be comprehended. Only when the town is so small as to be in itself a neighborhood do the two concepts become married.

A city's park commission should review periodically, with its park department, their long-range goals for development so as to make certain that philosophy and concepts, as originally determined, are not put aside or glossed over in favor of tempting commercial schemes or narrow and unrelated purposes. In situations such as found in Los Angeles' Park Commission, which has continually promoted such antitheses to proper park planning as high-rise apartments and Disneyland-style chair lifts, consideration of prospective commissioners' experience and background should be made. Such citizens, serving often without compensation, need not be professional landscape architects, planners, recreation leaders, or naturalists. The average citizen, with no possibility of conflict of interest and possessing a willingness to contribute his time toward a better city, can serve with distinction. Appointments of a political nature, or for the purpose of giving balance to the commission, tend to lessen its function as a viable force for the city's welfare. Who should be appointed to the park commission? Public spirited citizens of course. But as a general guide to background of interest and knowledge which is applicable, the following kinds of talent should be considered: Landscape architect, civil engineer, elementary school teacher, naturalist, planner, architect, psychologist, public service official, religious official, high school coach, local businessman, mother (with young children).

Inasmuch as automobiles, parking lots, and the decline of public transportation in general have a definite adverse effect on our city parks, automobile dealers may not make ideal candidates for the park commission. Also suspect are realtors, land speculators generally, and various kinds of builders. The park commission must not be used as a political plum!

Finally, so as to aid commissions and departments in the determination of park policy and long-range goals, the following check lists are offered:

A. Separation of functions and facilities related to the:
1. Square Concept
2. Park Concept

What To Do

Square Concept	Park Concept
walking (to)	walking (from)
making noise	making quiet
gathering	dispersing
demonstrating	relaxing
active involvement	passive self-involvement
find your fellow man	find yourself
get the news	forget the news
buy things	make things
watch	do
make propositions	make proposals
shop	plop

What To See

Square Concept	Park Concept
dressed up people	barely dressed people
dogs on leash	birds and squirrels
heightened and accentuated urban surroundings	contrasts with urban surroundings
waiter and tables	picnic on the grass
statues	trees
dramatic fountains	bubbles and drippings
geometric basins	natural ponds, streams
important civic structures	half hidden toilets
pigeons	robins
pretty girls	pretty girls

B. In addition to the very different functions practiced in park and square, the following list of facilities associated with parks suggests levels of priority to be considered for major parks:

swimming pool	high (depending upon any systemized location for city-wide coverage)
zoo	high (see foregoing comments)
garden exhibits	high (see following chapter)

amphitheatre or portable stage — high (see foregoing comments)

play areas with fixed equipment — high

boating — high (sail, paddle, oar, or low h.p. electric motors)

skating—ice — high

roller — medium (some good outdoor circuits exist)

grass play fields — high (especially if flexible as to use)

specific periodic city organized activities:

festivals — high

carnivals — high

concerts — high

fairs — high

picnic areas — high (avoid structures, paved surfaces, and other low-maintenance features likely to reduce essential qualities of picnicking)

hiking, nature paths, etc. — high

bicycle trails — high (careful designing is important)

tennis and other surfaced court games — medium (best reserved for neighborhood parks)

golf — medium (space requirements are a major consideration. The expanding pressure for public courses may result in creating separate courses outside the parks.)

museum — medium (best located on park's edge. Amsterdam has street entrance and projects into park with outdoor sculpture garden. An effective transition.)

restaurant — medium (keep under strict control of park department)

conservatory, greenhouses — medium (depending upon structure, purposes)

clubrooms, meeting houses — medium (best reserved for neighborhood parks)

horse trails — medium (if already located elsewhere)

lawn bowling — medium (space and cost of help are factors. Devotees usually pay for maintenance.)

scientific, academic foundations	low (depending on breadth of public involvement)
schools	low (the advantage of location favors the school, not the park)
library	low (the green areas surrounding some city libraries—Los Angeles and New York—suggest park setting. Like museums, keep on the park's edge.)
race courses—horse	low
auto	nonconforming
amusement centers	low (commercial-spectator type belong elsewhere)
large auditoriums, sports stadiums, arenas	nonconforming
housing projects	nonconforming
police academies, target ranges, etc.	nonconforming
hospitals and sanitariums	nonconforming

While such suggestions for priorities should prove helpful in planning the growth and development of a major city park, or in re-organizing a park system, final decision for any specific park planning program is dependent upon local needs and conditions. The direct line of responsibility for determining precedents and park design policy is as follows:

Park Commission (appointed)
Park Department (hired)
Mayor and Council (elected)

For many smaller cities, the park department's budget does not allow for retention of sufficient professional personnel on staff. In such cases when major park development is contemplated, it is absolutely necessary to acquire outside consultation, such as:

Landscape Architect
Architect
Civil Engineer
Horticulturist
Recreation Leader

Most communities, no matter how small, should be able to locate professionals as well as other talented individuals who can greatly assist in the development and enrichment of the city's parks and recreational programs. In terms of instructional recreation, it is sometimes advisable to first find out what kind of talent sources can be tapped. Thus evening and summer programs can be developed in such widely varied pursuits as: Flower arranging, musical instruction, ceramics, puppet theatre, life drawing, "slow-pitch" softball (for over thirties), model airplanes, tennis instruction, and many, many others, including neighborhood action programs aimed at stabilizing the community.

Design, the last of four major factors of park planning, is thus represented by a variety of considerations, including of course, in its final stage of development, a drawing on paper—a master park plan, which represents the collective thinking of city planners, civic leaders, elected officials, recreation advisors and neighbors. It is translated into graphic form as a working plan, by landscape architects under the park department's jurisdiction. Now, in the hands of competent designers, the criteria for successful development can be organized, arranged, and formed into a well-ordered physical plan. No amount of explanation or do-it-yourself park designing should be attempted here, since the variety of problems and technical knowledge involved are so great.

IDENTIFYING BASIC PARK PROBLEMS

While increasing urban population and lengthening leisure time make the acquisition of close-in land for new park development most necessary, the renovation of established parks is also needed and immeasurably less difficult to accomplish. New design concepts, in view of modern social organization and habit, should be applied to existing parks to enhance efficiency of use. In many instances, changes wrought by modern society have had deleterious effects on parks, bringing various kinds of encroachment, nonconforming use, and imprisonment by safety standards along with technological advances.

A few such problems are discussed herein with appropriate examples.

A. Vehicular Penetration
   Examples: Villa Borghese (Rome)
             Balboa Park (San Diego)
             Elysian Park (Los Angeles)

Most major parks today necessarily incur vehicular intrusion. The danger develops when such a park becomes so intersected by through traffic as to be appreciably reduced in use and effectiveness. The important word here is "through." In the proper development of large city parks, designers often find it necessary to introduce some automobile access, such being a realistic view of urban life today. It will be dependent upon the designers to so integrate this access into the plan as to insure against inherent dangers of vehicular encroachment and spatial interruption. But it can be demonstrated at the outset that traffic *to* the park—terminal traffic—is a far different prospect than *through* traffic. In the former, the pace of travel is leisurely, the park being a goal not a momentary visual interlude. Traffic engineers, however, seem to be at a loss over how to handle through traffic. Sometimes high speed and heavy flow are discouraged by the use of curves which conform to the park's design, reduce speed, and promote greater safety. Rome's finest park, Villa Borghese, suffers incredibly from a maze of through traffic, most of which is forced to conform to such a solution involving a nerve-wracking series of tight curves and narrow pavement. The resulting parade of braking, shifting, and honking autos shatters the park's tranquility without any compensation to the park. The argument for wide, straight boulevards through parks claims to expedite traffic and avoid congestion. In the case of Elysian Park, Los Angeles, the major route to Dodger Stadium bisects the park with six lanes of high-speed roadway. It has proven to be so convenient that commuters now use it as a short cut between the two freeways which border the park. Thus it can be argued that, while twisting, narrow streets create noise and congestion through the park, expressways encourage traffic that would never have developed otherwise. However, any vehicular access through the park invites noise, danger, and limitations in the park's flexibility. San Diego's Balboa Park, once the West's largest contiguous city park, has been twice violated by major highways, greatly reducing the force and potential capabilities of this once majestic park.

Golden Gate Park suffers less from such direct through traffic. With one or two exceptions, its vehicular accesses are intended to serve park visitors; but in so doing, overly provide for such, creating a paradise for park viewers to the detriment of users. In summation, the specific dangers of vehicular penetration include:

1. Danger to pedestrians, park users.
2. Limitation to pedestrian accesses.
3. Introduction of undesirable noise.
4. Limitation on park's capabilities.
5. Weakening of park's potential as an organizing agent.

B. Nonconforming Functions
Examples: Villa Borghese (Rome)
Golden Gate Park (San Francisco)

Already described previously, nonconforming facilities and activities represent a threat to park stability. Villa Borghese, for a century a dumping ground for all manner of public and private endeavor, can again be cited as a leading example. Here are found three race tracks, two foreign academies, three museums, a college, and various private facilities, all of which tend to reduce the overall effectiveness of the park.

Nonconforming uses can be dangerous as well as wasteful and inappropriate. Children playing in Elysian Park in Los Angeles often bring home tear gas cannisters from the Los Angeles Police Department target range—located in the park! A certain percentage of these fail to explode, and if undetected by maintenance crews they become a serious hazard to park users. In January, 1972, a six-year-old youngster lost his right hand after a tear gas cannister, which he found in the park, exploded at his touch. It is difficult to comprehend any rationalization on the part of the park commission in continuing to permit such a dangerous as well as nonconforming activity within a park system which they are obliged to protect. Yet the problem grows larger. On November 7, 1972, the Los Angeles taxpayers were asked by the Mayor and City Council to *increase* the size of the Police Department activities now improperly housed in Elysian Park. The argument raised against the measure read in part, as follows:

Parks In Danger!
Vote 'No' on U

Elysian Park is once again in danger—real danger.

During the past seven years the Citizens Committee to Save Elysian Park, a volunteer group backed by thousands of people, has fought off numerous attempts to grab pieces of the park for non-park purposes in violation of the City Charter—notably 63 acres for a trade show and convention center, 77 acres for an oil drilling lease, more acres for a multi-lane freeway link.

Now the 575-acre park, second largest in Los Angeles and one of the most beautiful in the entire country, is threatened with the loss of 21 acres for a new Police Academy to be built in conjunction with the existing facility.

In voting to place Proposition U on the ballot, the City Council majority brushed aside a study by the City Administrative Officer (CAO) which the Council itself had requested. It likewise rejected the recommendation of its own Joint Committee (Recreation and Parks, and Police, Fire and Civil Defense), which proposed that the Police be asked to secure a new site for the Academy and vacate the present site in Elysian Park within three years. The detailed, 59-page report of the CAP contained the following basic conclusions:

1. The Elysian Park site is now and will always be inadequate for the high quality and comprehensive training required for the Los Angeles Police Department.
2. The continuing development of Elysian Park under both the Recreation and Parks Master Plan, and the current Emergency Employment Act watering program, will result in increased public use of the park surrounding the academy site. This will result in constant irritation and is an incompatible use of public land.
3. There are several viable and attractive alternative sites which would provide the Los Angeles Police Department with a better facility at which to train the recruits and provide firearms and other types of specialized training.
4. A consolidated recruit training program with the Sheriff could offer a substantial reduction in City training costs. . . .*

The argument *for* the initiative was one of cost. However, the official cost estimate done by the City, which included land values as well as construction, showed that the Elysian Park plan would be more costly to the City than any of four alternate city-owned sites. The real reason for continued usurpation of park land by the Police Department of Los Angeles is, not surprisingly, the surrounding amenities of the park itself. Police morale, which includes *exclusive* use of such park facilities as tennis courts, handball courts and a swimming pool, was cited as the basic reasoning for the Elysian Park location. On November 7, 1972, the police got their wish. Another 21 acres was taken from the park. Public indifference made all the difference.

Golden Gate Park, one of the oldest city parks in the western United States, likewise suffers as a "culture dump." More recently, the park commission has demonstrated better judgment. Additions, such as Strybling Gardens, greatly improve the park's value to the city. By adopting a priorities check list, which in turn is derived from a predetermined policy, park commissions can avoid

nonconforming activities despite pressure from the short-sighted, the ill-informed, and the profit-takers.

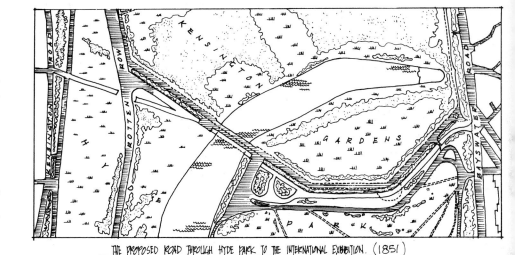

THE PROPOSED ROAD THROUGH HYDE PARK TO THE INTERNATIONAL EXHIBITION. (1851)

C. Isolation by Major Thoroughfares
    Examples: Hyde Park (London)
    Elysian Park (Los Angeles)

Freeways, high-speed arterials, or densely traveled thoroughfares which border parks tend to isolate them from their immediate surroundings, unless sufficient pedestrian access is provided. Lacking over- or under-passes, such access is limited to major intersections, which are often far apart in the case of large parks. Crossing a major thoroughfare, in the middle of the block or at the junction of streets terminating at the thoroughfare, is dangerous and should be discouraged by design. City officials, as a rule, decline to place boulevard stops or signal lights anywhere short of major intersections for the sake of avoiding congestion build-up. Hyde Park, London, offers easy pedestrian access on only two sides. Along

*Citizens Committee to Save Elysian Park.

Park Lane where entrance is frustrated, the park is less frequently used, its major value being visual relief to the motorist. Hyde Park and its contiguous neighbor, Kensington Gardens, suffered further abuse by nonconforming activities long before Dodger Stadium in Los Angeles' Elysian Park. An 1862 drawing (illustration) shows a road through both parks proposed as a means of handling traffic to the International Exhibition held in Hyde Park. Elysian Park, like many western city parks, is almost unreachable except by automobile. Even so, access of any kind is severely limited on the east and south by freeways. It is possible to somewhat reduce the audial and visual encroachment of adjacent high-speed traffic by substantial earth moving, mass planting, and block walls; however, these practices tend to increase the tendency toward isolation, giving the park the appearance of turning its back on the community. Like great private estates, we might expect to be greeted by padlocked gates and large unfriendly dogs. In the hands of a competent park designer, such problems of isolation and penetration can be properly resolved. Generally, it should be noted simply that city parks require easy access and need be designed to encourage such. *A park's very existence depends upon its being used.*

D.   Outdated, Inappropriate Design
      Examples: Luxembourg Gardens (Paris)
                 Regent's Park (London)

Countless examples exist, including the many pathetic "memorial" parks, converted fairgrounds, and inherited estates; but to make

the point most objectively, two of Europe's most familiar parks are cited for illustration. It would be difficult to find a more popular park in Europe than the Luxembourg Gardens of Paris. Located in the densely populated sixth arrondisement along the Boulevard St. Michele, this grand old park receives heavy usage indeed. It is the backyard for the children of the district, and serves as well for the Sunday Promenade. It is formal and dignified, but due to the inflexibility of its design, ill-equipped to meet growing and changing recreational needs. Toy boats can be sailed in the very formal and imposing *grande bassin,* and children's sandboxes have been tucked unobtrusively between the rows of formal sculpture along the Observatoire—the finger park which leads into the gardens—but such efforts as these, always subordinate to the overriding theme, appear pathetically inept. They serve only to demonstrate the need for new thinking in park design as well as to point out the futility of patchwork solutions. So the measure of past values remains, forcing today's park needs to conform to solutions for the past. Historic works should be preserved, but a park or garden which was never intended for public use cannot be expected to accommodate the people—today or in any age.

Regent's Park, London, enjoys similar popularity mainly due to its excellent close-in location, size, and high quality of maintenance. Although this park likewise was intended originally for royalty, there remains here a much higher degree of flexibility due mainly to John Nash's visionary plan; and as a result, succeeds to a greater extent in providing a base for today's recreational uses. London's zoo is here, as are numerous floral works, playing fields, and, unfortunately, two colleges. The Royal Promenade (Broadwalk) is, however, ill-suited to contemporary use (save for parades and demonstrations), as are the inner circle, queen's gardens, and various other bits of memorabilia. Throughout this great park, its arbors, idyllic lagoons, "Gardenesque" plantings, and romantic sculpture lives the sweet nostalgic presence of England's recent glorious past. Regent's Park, by all measure—location, shape, size, design—is a successful park. But like most of London's royal parks as well as many of the major parks of larger European cities, it suffers the fate of a museum piece. It's understandable. The age of reason brought Europe to a social and cultural crescendo—reflected in the architecture, gardens, and major cities of the continent. In the following century, industrial might gave Europe the muscle to expand her far flung empires. Small, colorful wars of simple design amidst ascending nationalism everywhere mark this period as one of smug, self-satisfaction and unabashed vigor. The wealthy and titled enjoyed life immensely while the cities grew black with the grime of factories. It was la vie en rose for Europe—her last period of singular pre-eminence. Emerging from 50 years of chaos and fear, it is understandable to see her cling to the reminders of the rose-colored years. But there is no more room in her cities for museums; and parks—like the cities themselves—are living elements, vital organs of the cities' total well being.

In Germany, the Netherlands, and the Scandinavian countries, the bright, positive new look of Europe is reflected in their city parks. While American designers continue to struggle with Olmstedian vs. "new geometric" concepts, the planners in Stockholm, Amsterdam, Stuttgart, and Helsinki are searching for ways to effect total integration between the physical components of the urban environment—while reaching out for sociological and psychological help as well in creating a recreational balance to improve the emotional climate for urban man.

Such severe physical problems as commutation congestion, population sprawl, unstructured and amorphous patterns of growth, destructive commercialism, air and water pollution, and other ills inherent to an urban structure still evolving from an agricultural economy beset most major cities of the western world. Must cities destroy themselves—stew in their own putrid juices until nothing remains but a fetid residue? It has happened before. Rome lay desolate for over two hundred years, her population reduced to one tenth its earlier size. Pestilence, contamination, fear, and mistrust reduced her to decay and desolation. Not war. Today tribes of educated young people are fleeing the cities to erect new societies in what remains of virgin America. Like the countless numbers who fled ancient Rome to find something better, they are in a sense rejecting the best that the modern city can offer, including war.

The terrible destructive forces unleashed on Europe's cities in World War II have resulted, however, in some exciting and creative new concepts in planning. For those who love cities and believe them to be man's greatest achievement and best hope for peace and progress, the examples of Rotterdam and Coventry are hopeful signs of man's indomitable spirit and ability to achieve greatness. It can even be accomplished without willful military destruction, as Stockholm and Paris will testify. On the one hand, almost total destruction of these ancient cities has resulted in vigorous new development and fresh, contemporary look. Even a stronger case in point is Hiroshima, which today features a "peace park" to commemorate the city's victory over the forces of blind destruction. Lacking any advantages wrought by bombing, Stockholm has, nevertheless, forged a dynamic 20th Century image of the ideal city—complete with a revolutionary concept of parks and parkways. Paris, too long emersed in the 19th Century, is now actively involved in a greater Paris new town master plan. Though late in starting, there is the advantage of studying results in London, Stockholm, and Amsterdam as well as the American cities' suburban sprawl.

Here in our American cities, the danger signs which point to urban chaos are clear. The problem then is not merely to understand them, but to act—before our eyes, ears and throats become too clogged to see, hear and cry out.

Geneva. Parc Anglais.   The park is a frame, a container for the celebrations of the people therein. They give it scale, and in return the park gives them status.

Stuttgart. Schlossgarten.

Stuttgart. Schlossgarten.

Athens. A neighborhood park.

Geneva. Parc Anglais.

London. Trafalgar Square.

London. St. James's Park. . . The greatest measure of a city park is in the degree to which it permits people to seek themselves—and in its appeal to all ages.

Stockholm, Millesgarden.

Stockholm. Tantolunden Park. (Courtesy Gosta Glase.)

Stockholm. Ralambshovsparken. (Courtesy Parkavdelningen.)

Stockholm... Art and theatre in the park. From the sublime to the bizarre. The magnificent works of Carl Milles, contemporary abstract forms, whimsical works, erotic posters, and painting displays all find space within the city's liberal park system. The scrawl wall and the porta-stage are probably Stockholm firsts.

Stockholm.

London. St. James's Park.   On resting. The park is a place to sit or lie down on a fine day. Feel the sun on your face on a chilly day or the cool breezes on a warm one. Feel all the elements about you. Feel the grass with your toes. Notice how the earth yields under you—as paved surfaces never do.

Such a place within the city, such a park gives us a chance to investigate our surroundings and ourselves. Here one can ponder life's destiny, plan an activity or read a book. Alone. There is something frightening in our society today which works to prevent solitude. (Courtesy Peter Blom.)

Paris. Bois de Vincennes.

Stockholm. Humlegarden. (Courtesy Peter Blom.)

Paris. Parc Buttes-Chaumont.

Paris. Bois de Boulogne.

Paris. Bois de Vincennes.

Stockholm. Blackeberg Playpark (Courtesy Gosta Glase).

PART 3
THE PARK SYSTEMIZED

THE PARK AS A NEIGHBORHOOD CATALYST

A city of more than neighborhood proportions should become, according to 17th Century architect Christopher Wren, a system of neighborhoods, each semi-dependent, semi-autonomous. Wren identified London's neighborhoods by means of community churches, each displaying its own unique spire rising high above its surroundings as a means of neighborhood identification, and acting as a catalyst for neighborhood-related activities. An architect of broad vision, Wren understood the danger inherent to amorphous, unscaled urban sprawl; and taking advantage of the great fire, recaptured in 17th Century London much of the humanism of that city, which had been disappearing since the middle ages—just as surely as any sense of human scale has largely disappeared in most American cities today.

Wren chose churches as the nuclei around which neighborhood complexes could emerge. One hundred years earlier, Sixtus V had attempted a restructuring of sprawling Rome by identifying urban nodes and then emphasizing them by deliberate design. Sixtus had hoped to tie the various major elements of the city together—as Wren was to do in London later—by first separating points of activity and then relating them by visual means to one another in terms of an overall system.

While Wren considered churches to be the strongest and most logical tool for this function, Sixtus used the Piazza. With its tremendous potential for organization and its particular appeal to

Roman temperament, the open piazzas of Baroque Rome became a new symbol of urban scale for the Western world. Each such space offers its own drama as well as a new choice of direction or stopping place. Adjoining piazzas could be visually telegraphed—an important design aspect which enabled the entire system to remain dynamic, charged with the sense of linkage and tension. Sixtus identified these nodes by means of Egyptian obelisks of varying sizes and embellishment. These are seen to serve as pylons for the organization of traffic and in aesthetic terms, to provide a sensitive balance between vertical and horizontal themes. Like giant, urban-scaled exclamation points, they continue to identify major civic spaces today as they have since the 16th Century.

Planners and architects have long understood the purposes behind the efforts of such men, as they have likewise grasped the meaning and value of the agora concept of ancient Athens. By the middle of the 19th Century, Ruskin was discussing the purpose and form of structured urban space, while Haussmann, Nash and others were developing these concepts in the realities of their place and time. Such efforts to achieve moment continue today as witnessed by Stockholm and particularly in the new towns of Tapiola, Reston, and Cumbernauld.

As should be evident, the city parks have a similar part to play in the organization of the city. If churches formed the common basis of neighborhood organization in 17th and 18th Century

London, then perhaps neighborhood parks can be seen as providing that basis of commonality for the more leisurely oriented cities of 20th Century America.

True, the apparent desire among many Americans for separation and compartmentalization, which brought on the automobile and the single-family residence, remains a strong force in shaping the taste and judgment of American life. Further indulgences, however, in decentralization and depersonalization may prove to be catastrophic. The drive-in neighborhood park, including drive-in picnic facilities, is already a ludicrous reality as the nation continues to be plagued by the spread of "bubblemania"—that mental aberration which causes us to maintain a screen against each other, against the ideas, love, fears, and anxieties of those with whom we might come in contact. We wrap our goods in plastic swathing to prevent any possibility of contamination; and likewise, we wrap ourselves behind glass and plastic—to see, but not be affected by those around us. See-through clothes and tiny skirts may be an attempt to bridge the chasm; but more likely, they derive from bubblemania—look and savor but don't reach out to touch the body or mind beneath.

The growing social revolution among young people in this country and Europe today seems fully cognizant of the vertical and horizontal stratification of their elders; and through the phenomena of the teach-in, love-in, be-in, happening, theatre of confrontation and countless other experiments in social restructuring, many are seeking to find ways to build true urbanity into the decaying framework of our cities. Such a renaissance of public spirit has not been seen to develop in stratified suburbia any more than in the inner city jungles. However, it can and does take place in the park. Older neighborhoods that really are identifiable as such make significant use of the parks with which they are associated. Even drab, poorly maintained neighborhood parks have been consistently more successful than better developed suburban parks where adjacent lots are a half acre or more. (Furthermore, middle class residents are often suspicious of the park's habitues.)

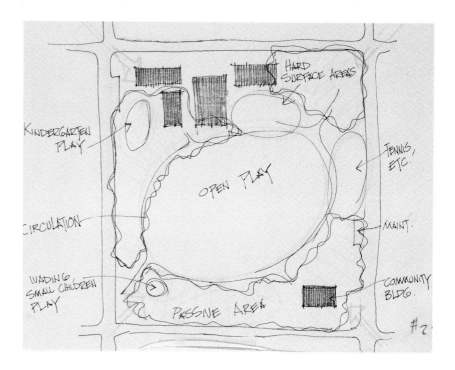

The illustration indicates common uses deriving from the park-school combination. The facilities of primary concern to the school program are more directly related to the school itself, and those facilities of little or no use to the school are furthest removed. The open center is an all-purpose common space and acts in a transitional capacity.

Thus elementary school and neighborhood park are seen as possessing mutually beneficial facilities—a symbiotic relationship which should be recognized. The school is of walking distance, in most instances, for the children and likewise for their parents. As such, it serves as the center for a variety of neighborhood events, from Christmas plays to home-grown carnivals. Problems of maintenance and security need to be worked out between the school board and the park commission to preserve a spirit of cooperation throughout.

The final design for any neighborhood park should be based

on specific requirements of the residents but it will normally be found best to keep a flexible open center with heavy use areas and structures grouped efficiently near perimeters. For older or changing neighborhoods, renovation, removal of streets, and purchase of adjacent property may sometimes save a hapless park; but unfortunately the reverse has been a far more common occurrence. MacArthur Park in Los Angeles, a neighborhood park of significant local importance, was severely reduced in size and function a few years ago by the intrusion of Wilshire Boulevard. To facilitate auto traffic, the park was bisected, thus destroying the design concept and creating two less effective small parks in its place.

In East Los Angeles, two neighborhood parks have been continually in danger of being sold by the city in order to raise needed revenues. And these are parks which enjoy heavy local use! Countless examples of neighborhood park desecration can be cited. Racism, political strife, congregation by so-called undesirables and other factors of social confrontation, together with commercial greed, land grabbing interests, outcries for more parking lots, maintenance costs and such combine to imperil established parks and retard development of new parks. In order to remain a viable, cohesive nucleus, the neighborhood park must be made to function in accord with the needs and disposition of its residential surroundings.

Neighborhoods differ considerably in size and character, and the park should reflect this. There are, however, staple facilities which are found to be desirable in most neighborhood parks. Below are listed the seven commonly accepted basic physical elements for neighborhood park development.

1. Central open space, usually in grass, for flexible use— especially seasonal play. The central open space is the primary agent for design integration and flexibility. Open space also becomes very important in a neighborhood of apartments and crowded little houses.

2. Passive area, usually includes some places for picnicking, but should avoid paving and overstructuring. Use of trees preferred. People usually don't picnic in the rain anyway. Some benches will do. Lots of people prefer grass with a bit of natural separation produced by trees and shrubs.

3. Community building, if school facilities are not available. This is a *must* for the neighborhood park. It permits year round activity and should provide as minimal requirements a game or crafts room, one or two smaller meeting rooms, recreational office, storage room, and toilets.

4. Depending upon the needs of the neighborhood, some specific game facilities as shuffleboard, tennis, and bocce. The neighborhood should have a voice in this before plans are developed.

5. Spray or wading pool for five-year-olds and under. Very shallow, no railing required. This facility can be quickly drained when no recreation leader is on duty.

6. Hard surface fixed play area for younger children. The surfacing material under swings and jungle gyms may vary from decomposed granite to blacktop. Recent success with rubberized paving, outdoor carpeting and synthetic grass should be noted by park personnel. Reducing of skinned knees and bumped heads is always a worthy goal.

7. Some hard surface pavement for a variety of uses, as hopscotch, tricycle riding, roller skating, and various ball-bounce games.

Of course, many other additions will improve and individualize a park to better fulfill the specific neighborhood needs. Flower beds may be desired or even vegetable plots as independent projects. Sculpture, as a memorial or for its own sake, gives such a park singular distinction from all others. Nearby schools of art are loaded with eager and talented kids who would devote hours to sculpture projects for the cost of materials. Not having a downtown plaza, with dignity and prestige to maintain, the local park leaders and the people of the neighborhood might indulge themselves in a regular schedule of outdoor art display.

But whatever facilities are under consideration, park personnel should carefully avoid those which would tend to remove the park from neighborhood classification. Unless every neighborhood park builds a swimming pool, those that do immediately become city-wide parks. Unlike the traditional single large park in this country, a system of secondary parks, each equally equipped, should be developed before impairing the function of the neighborhood parks. Such parks are thus seen to be unifying nuclei, replacing the church and the market place. Since the shopping center is usually located on the basis of cost and availability of land, it tends to become a destroyer of neighborhoods, much the opposite of its distant precedent. With the continuing increase of leisure time and the decreasing availability of land for single family residential development, the priorities of the neighborhood park as a community organizer should be obvious.

In the hierarchy of neighborhood parks, the tiny vest-pocket park or neighborhood commons acts for a single block in the way that the larger park acts for the overall neighborhood. These tiny parks may be simply vacant or condemned lots, the building having been removed to allow for some relief from structural monotony. Legislation has been introduced as early as 1958 to allow for the creation of such micro-parks in newly developed housing tracts merely by reducing minimum lot sizes and combining these savings in the form of unbuilt lots throughout the development. A home owner's organization, with some park department help, can be responsible for the design and development. In neighborhoods of younger families, such parks become known as "tot lots," and as such provide primarily for the preschool children of the immediate area. But they can be developed with swimming pools and other adult recreational facilities so as to relieve the pressure of backyard development. Where yards are small—as well as landscaping budgets—the advantage of such mini-parks is clear.

By and large, the vest-pocket park, by any name, is more a product of afterthought than systematic planning. The fact that it has occurred at all is an indication of overall failure, not only in systemized park planning, but systemized long-range residential planning itself. Vest-pocket mini-parks are a result of lot lines and residential sterility. In this age of increasing outer awareness and inner identity crisis, the need for greater involvement in public and community activity is clearly becoming critical. The lessons to be learned by the Renaissance Pleasure Faire in Los Angeles, the Woodstock Festival in New York, and countless other episodes of youthful involvement must not be lost to middle-class and middle-aged America. They are trying to tell their elders to reassess their value standards, specifically in more human terms. They are providing lessons in cooperation between all types of people as well as the need to express individuality. But most of all, such massive encounters, often confused and discomforting, suggest a most fundamental human quality. "People who need people," as a popular song explains, "are the luckiest people in the world." The young *are* searching for identity. They recognize bubblemania as a divisive menace in the midst of our society, and have begun to search for a way back to community identity, even when that community is only artificial or momentary.

SYSTEMIZED HIERARCHY: A PARK FOR ALL SEASONS

Systemizing is basically a matter of organizing a method of determining need and priorities. The whole of park activities and purposes, like life itself, cannot be simplified and stratified into systems. The great threat of mechanization is that it aspires to be a tool and becomes a way of life.

The basic framework for any city park system is seen to include at least two major categories—the major park with its unique facilities and city-wide appeal, and the neighborhood park, nucleus for community activity and recreation, repeated according to formula throughout the city.

In addition, several other types of public parks are often found to be necessary, although they do not easily fit into either category. The following is a list of all types of parks in common use today in the city:

1. Primary Park (city-wide)
2. Secondary Park (neighborhood)
3. Specialized Park
4. Commons
5. Amusement Park
6. Green Square
7. Corridor Park
8. Super Park

1. *Primary Parks*—Already discussed earlier at length, this category is represented by city-wide parks of major proportions (100-1000 acres or more) which offer a variety of flexible and unique facilities (zoo, theatre), as well as most of the general facilities of neighborhood parks. A peculiarity of many American cities, as seen earlier, is the penchant for creating one large primary park (2000 acres or so), as in Philadelphia, St. Louis, and San Francisco. European cities are more likely to have several smaller sized parks of up to 500 acres each.

2. *Secondary Parks*—These are, of course, the neighborhood parks just described. They may vary in size from tot-lot or vest-pocket dimensions up to 40 or 50 acres. MacArthur Park, Los Angeles (33 acres) is an example of a heavily used neighborhood park representing a densely populated downtown residential area. Regardless of land cost, the close-in parks serving older or redeveloped high-density areas need to be larger to accommodate the heavier use. Downtown parks serve a greater need than those of the suburban fringe where low density, single family private yards prevail (as inadequate substitutes). In New York, Los Angeles, Houston and many, if not all large cities of this country, low income minority neighborhoods are hard-pressed to acquire park sites, or where developed, to keep them properly maintained. Such important parks as Hazard (25 acres),

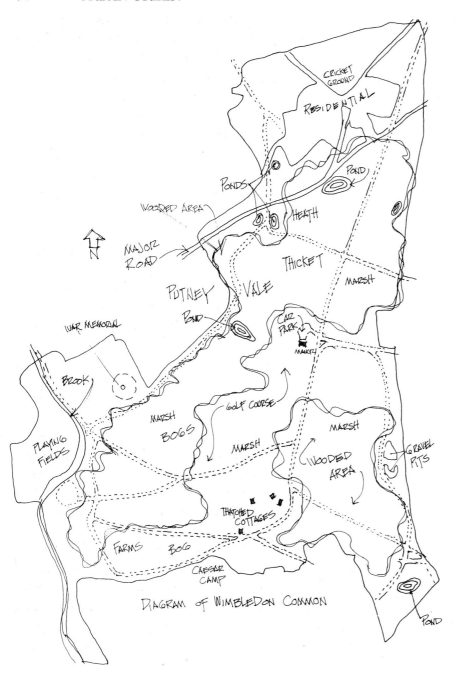

DIAGRAM OF WIMBLEDON COMMON

Lincoln (46), and Hollenbeck (21) in the close-in neighborhoods of Los Angeles are now badly suffering from official neglect. Beautiful Lincoln Park, with its stately old boathouse, which speaks eloquently of an earlier, more gracious setting, is today improperly maintained. The local residents, primarily Mexican-Americans, make little use of the boats; and for this reason, the fine old structure is scheduled to be torn down rather than be repaired. The parks department hopes a private concessionaire will build another one if it can be made a profitable venture!

3. *Specialized Parks*—There are a variety of narrow use or specialized park uses which are often best-suited to separate development—as special-use parks. A zoo by itself is considered as such. Arboretums and botanical gardens featuring native plants, tropicals or floral displays are considered to be specialized when other aspects of the park are kept subordinate to the dominant theme.

Organized sports, such as Little League baseball and Pop Warner football, can make use of specialized sport parks, and by doing so alleviate pressure on the neighborhood parks. Team efforts involve considerable equipment, noise, traffic, lighting, and seating. In Pomona, California, a neighborhood park has been completely overhauled for city-wide organized sports, with all the accompanying necessities, thus depriving the local people—Black and Mexican-Americans—of their park and their neighborhood identity. The sports park in Claremont, California, mentioned earlier, is a good example of a special-use park. Its narrow proportions and physical separation from the surrounding houses make it a poor choice for a neighborhood park site; but its near-central location makes it suitable for a special-use sports park, and its disadvantages have now proved to be beneficial. The adjacent neighborhood has its own park just down the street, and all of the city's neighborhood parks are relieved of the necessity of providing regulation football and baseball fields. Other such specialized parks might include lawn bowling and shuffleboard courts, or whatever individualized function a city hopes to develop or protect. The important thing to remember is the distinctly separate role from that of the typical neighborhood park and the need to keep them apart and safe from the intrusions of one another.

4. *Commons*—As described in the first section, the traditional English Common derived from areas unsuitable for development—bogs and poorly drained hollows, or swales subject to washout during rainy periods. Having been set aside as such by royal proclamation, the commons served the public in a variety of ways, including grazing and farming. Today although still under marginal maintenance, they are more likely to resemble city parks. Huge Wimbledon Common retains much of its traditional spirit of wilderness, providing distinct advantages for the imaginative and adventuresome of all ages.

Boston Commons was conceived from the beginning as an open, natural park in the city's center—a gathering place for free citizens. It could be viewed as a public city park, predating London's first public parks by fifty years. In reality, Boston Commons evolves from the village green of New England's colonial towns. Park and square combined, the green probably represents the closest link in our times with the spirit and purpose of the agora of ancient Greece, where all men participated directly in the affairs of government.

Some such greens and commons still function in a related manner; but in most instances, the large, wooded tracts, preserved for centuries in unkempt splendor,

perform today as city parks. As a reminder of the ever present struggle to preserve open public space, witness this anonymous 18th Century English rhyme:

"The law condemns the man or woman
Who steals the goose from off the common,
But lets the greater robber loose
Who steals the common from the goose."

5. *Amusement Parks*—Amusement or pleasure parks are the antithesis of city parks, as they have been described herein. The pleasure park is no park at all but a carnival of commercial entertainment crowded into a few gravel, concrete or asphalt covered acres. In most cases, it is privately owned and controlled; and for this reason, plays only a related role in the city's park and recreation system. Some are well laid out, like famed Tivoli Gardens in Copenhagen, and have as a result become valuable to the city's overall well-being. Tivoli has been a successful Danish treat for a century; and even today, the charm and nostalgia of the '90's pervades the grounds. The success of Tivoli, Disneyland and other well-planned amusement parks is noteworthy; but their value to the public is largely limited to the narrow uses of commercial entertainment. The many values ascribed to parks and their uses are by and large frustrated in the merry-go-round and cotton candy world of amusement parks. While they admittedly have their values, the danger to public park systems becomes apparent when well-meaning but short-sighted park personnel attempt to translate Disneyland qualities into public park terms.

To obtain needed revenues, the Los Angeles Recreation and Parks Commission runs five golf courses in Griffith Park alone. Public outrage prevented the commissioner's plans to install tramways and other amusements as well; but the desire to create Disneylands in public parks continues to plague us. Again, the purpose of our parks must be stressed. They represent primarily *opportunity*. The very essence of spectator oriented commercialism must be scrupulously avoided so that the opportunity of self-involvement and exploration is made possible.

The amusement park usually lacks any real sense of open space—so essential to the public park. Apparently the owners simply cannot afford to allow large areas to remain idle; and as a result, the effect of most such commercial ventures is one of congestion, crowds, noise, and neon. It is the image of the city, not a retreat from it.

Los Angeles is not alone in being faced with creeping commercialism in parks. Among the worst examples which can be found in the Western World is Paris, where in the Tuilleries as well as in most Parisian parks, even the simplest of manually operated play equipment will cost toddlers the price of admission. From Bagatelle to Luxembourg Gardens a boulevardier will face the charge of a small fee just to sit and rest! It is most unfortunate to encounter modern-day commercialism in these beautiful historic grounds. And no matter how one chooses to measure culture, the true basis of any society's cultural growth can be found in its attitude towards its people's well-being. The concern for human dignity being expressed so explosively by America's young people today speaks more for this nation's cultural attainment than all of its youthful art and music. The latter are in fact reflections upon that new-found dignity rather than cultural achievements in their own right.

Likewise, Stockholm's emphatic efforts to dignify public spaces and facilities, and to broaden the extent of services to its people suggest the dynamic and productive quality of that city's cultural growth. To limit one's definition of a society's culture to the arts produced by few, while ignoring the quality of life endured is to assign outdated and stilted meanings to the word. The free zoo in St. Louis' Forest Park is far superior in layout, plantings, and wealth of exhibits to London's Regent Park Zoo—with its stiff entry fee. The psychological differences are even greater. One enters the Forest Park Zoo with a sense of appreciation and self-respect—a reassurance that the city really cares about its people.

In their desire to emulate the successes of Disneyland and, at the same time, sweeten the city's coffers, park commissioners are playing a dangerous game. The entire meaning of public trust and its future bearing on civic well-being may lie in the balance.

6. *The Green Square*—The most traditional of English city parks, the green square, is really not a park at all, predating the modern park concept described earlier by many centuries.

Originally associated with the late medieval plans of Oxford and Cambridge Universities, the ancestral green square was organized by the straight forward rectilinear placement of surrounding buildings. Entry was formally arranged through archways with secondary axes at the corners. The design was usually severe and unadorned. Medieveal college squares are closed spaces, unrelated spatially to each other, or larger surrounding enclosures.

In the city, the green square evolved during the 17th and 18th Centuries into a simply arranged, uncluttered rectangle, framed by trees and enclosed by residential terraces or civic buildings. More centrally located or openly planned, the green square of this period might have performed like the village green; but in fact its plan tended towards exclusion and a rejection of the principle of the gathering place.

Closed to most traffic, the green square is, nevertheless, ill-suited to use as a neighborhood park, its tradition being formal and passive, and the often haphazard placement of play equipment, backstops and horseshoe pits seem incongruous in these surroundings. The green square seems to exclude all but the immediate facing property—an unsatisfactory condition for many a neighborhood park.

Green squares, the reader will recall, vary from one-half block to several acres, but remain similar and somewhat limited in function. Linked to the past, their potential is not great without considerable evaluation as to function and relationship within the overall park system. Philadelphia's green squares function more like small parks and have as a result become much less sophisticated and more adaptable to contemporary use. Grosvenor Square in London, however, retains its traditional qualities of simplistic style and refined enclosure. With the American Embassy at its head, the square is formed by fashionable three-story terrace apartments facing across the long axis. The height and character of the embassy design were kept sympathetic to the older structures by its architect, Eero Saarinen. It lends emphasis, direction and balance to the overall scheme without danger of dominating it—a tribute to the skill of the architect. The postwar addition of the Roosevelt Memorial, on the other hand, is the singular unfortunate occurrence in that otherwise sublime spatial composition. It serves to prove how easily the delicate forces of balance can be offset in a spatial scheme.

London's Russell Square lacks this sophisticated directional frame, being dominated—and thus overbalanced—by the Victorian bulk of the Russell Square Hotel. The Square depends more on inner structure for success; and the contemporary design is generally effective, although modern-day English landscape architects have largely failed to master scale and spatial organization on a par achieved in the same degree as their predecessors.

7. *Corridor Parks*—In any re-evaluation of park systemization, the means by which physical linkage and, thereby, overall integration is made must be given highest consideration if that park system is to meet the challenge of the future. Planned, systemized linkage in every form must be studied for possible use in the struggle to harness the rampant, amorphous runaway growth of our cities.

Corridors of green can be envisioned as connectors between school and park, home and store, and, at the same time, as buffers which organize and shape a city's growth patterns, as safety devices and noise reducers, and as a means of linking together the city's parks. And they can do so much more. Pedestrian ways, riding and bike trails, can be made to connect throughout the city as in Stockholm, where her citizens can hike for miles through natural greenery with scarcely a glimpse of surrounding city-scape. By retaining the natural ridges and valleys within the city, Stockholm's planners have made us aware of the structure and scale of the immediate surroundings. It is not necessary to hike the ridges and forested corridors to appreciate the sense of humanizing organization they bring to the city.

Examine the corridors which already exist in any urban complex—valleys, ridge lines, waterways, freeways, parkways. In sprawling, low-density cities like Los Angeles and Houston, freeway parks can be developed. With the freeway acting as a corridor and separator as well—its hundred-foot rights-of-way banked in greenery—the addition of nodal parks can be readily envisioned. Just as off-ramps lead vehicles to surface streets, they could as well be employed in the development of such adjacent parks, which would serve much the same function as highway rest stops. During peak travel time or periods of heavy congestion, motorists could choose to pull off into these parks to await traffic thinning. Reading the paper or resting under a tree seem much better alternatives to waiting out traffic jams.

For the most part, freeways have proven to be destructive to existing neighborhoods far beyond the thoughts of route planners. Time after time such routes have been directed through the nuclei of neighborhoods, resulting in the destruction of a delicate organic balance, often many years in developing. Human communities, like plant communities, are often too subtle in their patterns of growth and relationships to be recognized as such by city planning officials, and like many a fragile ecological culture, are bulldozed into oblivion. Nothing much good will grow on our bladed slopes after the topsoil and drainage patterns have been destroyed. The same is true for sociological cultures, where patterns of development have been ruthlessly uprooted. But it need not have happened this way. If, for instance, the freeway systems with their accompanying swaths of green could have been planned to support existing neighborhood patterns by strengthening natural divisions and avoiding the dissection of nuclei—if such routes had been planned to go under or around rather than through the centers, a whole new concept for sprawling, low-density cities might have emerged. Ebenezer Howard envisioned such when he exploded the tight, high-density urban development of English cities, introducing air, light and greenery. Writing in 1898, his plan for a new "garden city" was almost immediately recognized and acted upon, resulting in the model cities of Welwyn Garden City and Letchworth—both north of London. Howard's work led to exploratory greenbelt new towns in United States during the depression years and was undoubtedly influencial in Frank Lloyd Wright's "Broadacre City." But any updating of the Garden City concept would necessarily have to take into consideration overriding problems of population and technological growth—especially since Howard's concept today is all too often translated into suburban sprawl with all of its ensuing problems of commuter transit systems. Such systems can be planned to enclose rather than penetrate identifiable community nuclei (as in the example of Lucca) if those responsible for their development would rearrange their priorities in favor of community stability rather than commuter expedience. Unfortunately many urban planners in America have apparently never thought of cities as places in which to live.

Natural corridors, such as water fronts, rivers, watershed valleys, ridgelines and arroyos, should be viewed as potential urban organizing agents. The Danube River divides Budapest into two distinctly different urban subcultures which, to a lesser degree, is also true of the river development in Paris, New York, and St. Louis. In Rome the banks of the Tiber, called lunga, have the potential in this more compact, crowded city of becoming effective pedestrian oriented corridor parks. Their present use, as high-speed traffic routes, is illogical and wasteful, especially in light of the dramatic bends taken by the river as it meanders toward the sea. It is much the same error as that committed by New York several years ago in erecting the Hudson River Parkway; but at least, it can be said of Rome that plans are now being developed to convert the lunga traffic to subsurface motorways and subway lines.

Riverways and sloughs subject to flooding can be turned

to advantage in the development of a natural corridor park system, like Toronto's. After the terrible flood damage caused by Hurricane Hazel in 1954 the city, in conjunction with the provincial government of Quebec, created the Toronto and Regional Conservation Authority, whose major responsibility has been the development of a flood control system through the city's riverways. A major aspect of the plan has been the creation of a network of riparian greenways which follow along and contain the river channels. These greenways have been planned as corridor parks for public usage, and maintained in a natural state in order to attract and protect regional birds and wildlife.

Toronto's riparian parkway system includes, primarily, the Don and Humber Rivers' passage through the city to Lake Ontario. Similar noteworthy river corridor systems occur along Washington D.C.'s Rock Creek, and Cleveland's famous "emerald necklace" along the Rocky River and the tributaries of the Cuyahoga. Los Angeles, as pointed out earlier, must act soon to save what is left of its natural corridors (Arroyo Seco and Santa Monica Mountains).

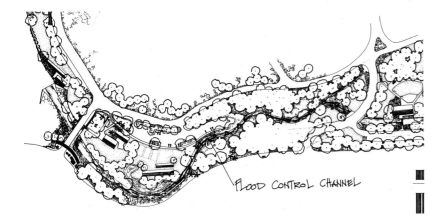

FLOOD CONTROL CHANNEL

Some fine examples of river front lineal park systems can be found along the Potomac River through Washington, D.C., the San Antonio River (mentioned earlier), and the Victoria Embankment stretching along the Thames River in London. The results in Washington and San Antonio are masterful examples of scenic resources used as organizing agents; but in London the potential of the Thames has never been realized.

With the decline of commercial river traffic, many cities whose original economy was based on river traffic are discovering, in the shifting fortunes of commerce, opportunities to redevelop decaying waterfront facilities. St. Louis has already made a grand start in that direction with the development of the Jefferson Memorial Park, a narrow river front strip which acts as a base for the great arch. Unfortunately the total effect will remain incomplete until the scruffy, soot-belching Illinois bank sees fit to follow suit.

Receding river commerce in Philadelphia has also led to river front park studies. Closely related to the ambitious new residential developments around Society Hill, the Delaware River front offers a clear opportunity for continued expansion of residential-recreational development, including plans for high-rise apartments, a marina, and pedestrian oriented parkways. San Francisco's Golden Gateway development, while primarily residential, is another example of waterfront renovation; and in Sacramento a very ambitious river front park system is nearing completion. By combining a variety of public and private facilities along the American River, the city and county park departments, working in conjunction with public-spirited citizens' groups, have managed to create a continuous river front park system through the center of the city. In so doing, they have made an unprecedented step toward re-evaluation, in human terms, of natural corridors in all cities.

Like the rivers and the hills which nurture and protect them, the cities are themselves naturally conceived and organically developed. Salvation and protection of un-polluted natural corridors and the creation of man-made pedestrian linkage systems may well be a key to the survival of our shrinking oasis parks and to the survival of human qualities in our cities as well.

8. *Super Parks*—The wooded glades are deep and quiet. A strolling couple surprises a deer, which quickly fades back into the shadowy forest. Nearby the open sunny vales are crowded with Sunday soccer games, sun-bathers, and picnickers. Solitude, communion—the spiritual needs of man joined by the great, seemingly bound-less dimensions of the natural retreat within the city, whose size alone distinguishes it from any other major city park. It is truly the super park—the *bois, bos, bosque,* or urban wood which, because of its size, is seen to be an organizing force acting upon the city rather than the reverse.

As such, its value to sprawling, crowded metropoli is immeasurable. Not a central park fighting for survival against its noisy, commercial encroachments, the super park is the greenbelt, the green corridor, the *Yin* which frames, separates and balances the *Yang* of commercial, urbanistic forces.

It must be huge to be an effective counter-balance—like the Bois de Boulogne, Paris, which combined with the Bois de Vincennes represents about one-tenth of the city's total acreage. These two majestic parks, "the lungs of Paris," contain and shape the city from east to west and are themselves connected, in spirit, along the River Seine and the vie de Triomphe—the combination of ave-nues, parks, palaces and places which form the back-bone of the city. Super parks, like Bois de Boulogne, the Amsterdamse Bos, and Fairmount Park in Philadelphia, derive their shapes from natural order. No arbitrary rec-tangles created by a city's grid pattern of streets; but finding their shapes in the contours, rivers, ridges, and valleys, they impart to the city a sense of scale by deny-ing the disorienting and dehumanizing effects of amor-phous sprawl. Hills, mountains, forests and rivers lend scale and balance to adjacent cities. They possess quali-fied dimensions which are visually measurable, and by which an individual can orient himself.

An example of such natural organizing forces can be found in the vast, rectilinear spread of greater Los Angeles, in most parts of which the individual with his ant's eye view finds little or no means of orientation to direction or scale. But in the vicinity of the Santa Monica Mountains, which cut a wedge between old Los Angeles and the burgeoning San Fernando Valley, a very different spatial rationale is discovered. Here one feels a sense of containment, a respite from the awesome infin-ity of unrelieved rectilinear monotony. Looking up towards the green and brown stretches of Griffith Park, we are able to discern the physical organic limits of the city. In Philadelphia, Fairmount Park (4,000 acres) spreads out along the banks of the Schuylkill River mak-ing a distinct separation between the city and its west-ern suburbs. Between the Schuylkill, the Delaware River and Fairmount Park, Philadelphia is largely contained in a natural frame. This is perhaps what gives the city—despite a century of chaotic planning—the potential for future greatness. The city's recent noteworthy progress along the lines of natural development is a sign of encouragement.

In 1969 Los Angeles achieved some distinction as well

by adapting its first official master plan, and shortly afterwards completing a master plan for gigantic Griffith Park. Long overdue, both plans may lack the vitality and imagination necessary to make them immediately meaningful. A plan which is an attempt to satisfy everybody is often no plan at all. Sadly enough, the greater potential for overall systematic organization of this vital area seems to fall outside the grasp of the present city planners. Griffith Park, forming the eastern promentory of the Santa Monica range, overlooks the Los Angeles River Valley, and a system of natural forces, including Silver Lake, Arroyo Seco, Echo Park and Elysian Park. The entire system is linked naturally to the river valley and can be projected with little difficulty to the Civic Center, including the Music Center complex and the new Bunker Hill residential projects. Thus a magnificent natural greenway of vast proportions can be envisioned funneling into the heart of the city, giving it the organic base and identity through separation which it surely needs. No great imagination is necessary to comprehend such a system of natural priorities. It existed as such only a few short years ago; but its value was not understood, and its structure, consequently, has been eroded away by subsequent development.

Armed with her new master plans and backed by a dedicated effort to develop a modern rapid transit system, hope for a rebirth in civic identity may eventually occur. It has taken 50 years, however, for Los Angeles to develop a master plan for Griffith Park. Is there any reason to hope that the city will develop a sense of civic being in a shorter period?

Both Philadelphia and Los Angeles have bungled past opportunities for greatness in a headlong dash for mediocrity; but Philadelphia, at least, has always hung on to its potential by preserving the great park, central park-

way and historic squares. With its new plan including open central space, close-in residential projects, preservation and renovation of historic sections and riverfront development, Philadelphia is at last living up to its heritage; and William Penn's concept of a "green town" may yet become a reality.

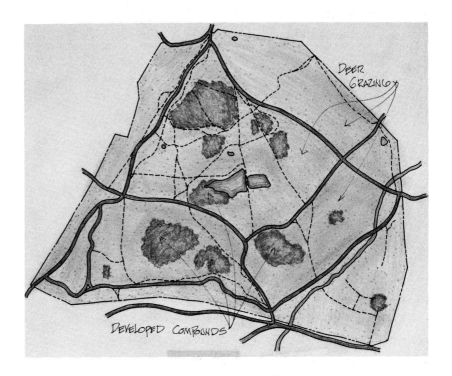

In London, Richmond Park, a huge natural area of some 2,500 acres in the south-western part of the city, acts in part as a game preserve as well as an urban organizing force. Too large to permit the kind of high maintenance preferred by the English, the designers have cordoned off "compounds" here and there—almost at random—for intense landscape treatment. These fenced-in enclosures appear like oases on an otherwise drab and underdeveloped plain. The total effect is disconcerting. One is almost forced to conclude that Richmond Park is too large for proper development—at least along the lines of its existing design practices. This would appear to be the result of a basic failure to grasp the scale and magnitude of the park's total function. Instead the designers chose to retreat—both physically and historically, and create therein the traditional little garden plots so dear to the English heart. Richmond's present design failure is not nearly so critical to London as it would be for any American city due to the wealth of large parks enjoyed by Londoners. It is a tribute to their sense of dignity and culture that they have so carefully guarded their royal inheritance of green spaces.

REPRESENTATIVE CITY PARK SYSTEMS

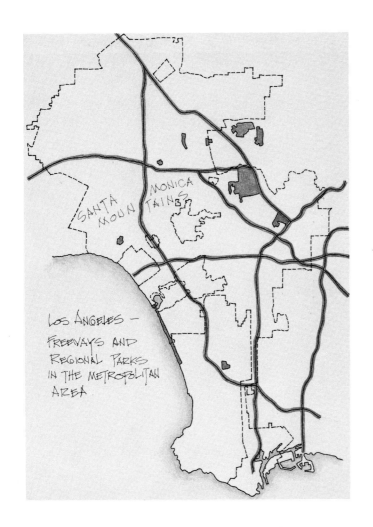

LOS ANGELES –
FREEWAYS AND
REGIONAL PARKS
IN THE METROPOLITAN
AREA

Cities resemble living organisms having a cellular structure, which includes growth, development and death. Such changes may affect the general health of the entire city if, for example, the death of a small park, local store or an established neighborhood is caused by and results in a replacement cell which is not beneficial. Change is recognized as an unimpeachable factor of urban life—something the Renaissance planners and Baron Haussmann may not have fully appreciated. It is the kind of change, however, which must be carefully observed. A park which becomes a parking lot, a neighborhood decimated by a freeway on-ramp, an adequate residential complex replaced by sterile and inadequate high-rise slabs, and a pleasant tree-lined avenue widened into a noise-filled commercial strip suggest changes which point towards galloping urban illness. Changes of this kind suggest cancerous growth, stagnation and decay. Death may be avoided for awhile just as trees with rotted centers continue to lead perilous, weakened lives by developing their cambium layers (suburbs); but unless remedial action is taken, death will surely result. A dead city with functioning but unrelated suburbs is like the fallen oak, rotting among its root suckers.

Besides its state of health, there is also a quality of life related to a city's character. This quality is part of a city's individuality and may be based on such factors as the particular richness of its cultural heritage, its economic history and present commercial status, its climatic, topographic and demographic development.

99

Until recently, it was still possible to detect the individual and differing qualities of Boston, New York, and Philadelphia. Unfortunately city planners in their zeal for expediency, and business entrepreneurs in their search for new markets have together managed to spread ubiquitous mediocrity across the face of America. Historic, ethnic and cultural distinctions have been wiped out by unimaginative planning practices and omnipresent orange-roofed eateries. In February of 1970, the famed Dodge House in Los Angeles fell to some sort of progress. Considered one of the fifteen most significant residences in the United States in terms of architectural merit and historic importance, Irving Gill's masterpiece was seen, by those forces of progress, as having outlived its usefulness. As change is inevitable, the Dodge House was as certain to reach extinction as Penn Station and those rapidly disappearing movie palaces of the 1930's. Even Chartres Cathedral, for that matter, has a finite life span. The point in question is not the saving of architectural relics for their own sake, as this would be opposing the biological and dynamic order of urban organics. The point in question is the *replacement*. St. Peter's Cathedral replaced an earlier structure by the same name, and Nero's magnificent palace was razed to make room for construction of the Coliseum. The Dodge House, as well, replaced something else. Now we would know what will replace the Gill masterpiece? Howard Johnson? Union Oil? Bank of America?

Individuality is surely dying in America. As these unique old relics disappear, sterile towers of monotony replace them, their fixed, tinted windows giving no hint of human scale functions behind them. San Francisco thus grows paler by the day as drab grey giants fill in her dramatic urban canyons and block majestic views. New glass and concrete boxes, coldly dehumanized in the fashion of modern technology, deprive New Yorkers of any feeling of relationship with their city. The older skyscrapers, with their regulated setbacks, individualized windows and refinement of detail, afforded some relief and sense of relatedness to the pedestrian below, notwithstanding the overriding sense of competitive ruth-

lessness one associates with this most artificially contrived of cities. The Statue of Liberty to the contrary, New York's Manhattan Island, suggests a gathering of wolves.

Twentieth Century urban ugliness is not exclusive to the United States. The clutter and chaos of unplanned commercial flotsom and jetsom swamp sedate old Guadalajara, threatening to completely obscure the stately urbanity of its 19th Century development. Montreal, once Canada's most unique city, is rapidly becoming a metropolis of architectural monotony; and in Brazil, São Paulo seems destined to outdo Chicago, Detroit, and Houston in search of urban mediocrity. History—if there is anyone to write it—may well mark the postwar years of the 20th Century as a period of technological debauchery, during which Western (and Japanese) man departed from his senses in a headlong search for ever-increasing services and universal civic sameness.

Is there any hope for our technology-riddled metropoli? Can today's industrial, expediency-inspired urban growth be controlled and redirected in accordance with natural and human factors? Perhaps such questions, at present anyway, must remain among the imponderables. We can, however, learn something from the ways cities have responded to technology and growth stimuli in the past. By a sampling of cities having widely varying physical park systems, it may be possible to make some basic observations about individual urban characteristics and the kind of physical park system they evoked.

London—The Swiss Cheese System

Owing to its garden-conscious populace, London remains one of the most park oriented of Western cities while, at the same time, suffering from a lack of any real overall city-wide urban organization. This makes the systemizing of parks a difficult task at best, insomuch as each park represents to the country-loving Englishman an oasis or, at best, a retreat from the noise and dirt of the surrounding city. Rather than effecting any sense of interrelationship, London's parks turn their backs on the city, becoming

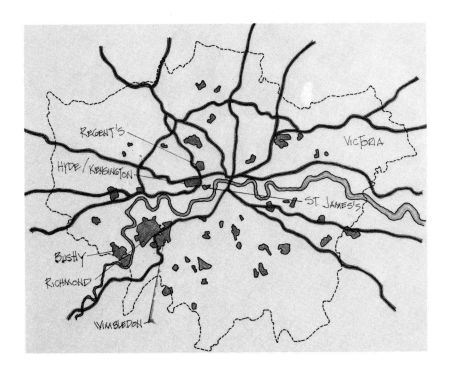

green refuges for the embattled citizenry. It is thus a swiss cheese park system with little attempt seen toward creating linkage. The exceptions are noteworthy, especially in their failure to accomplish the ends they sought. John Nash's attempt to link Regent's Park through a grand processional down Regent's Street to St. James' Park, and John Martin's vision of linking Central London's Royal Parks came to naught, although the physical relationship is readily apparent even today.

A forthright, all-encompassing approach to park systemization in London has been lacking despite the abundance of green open space. Natural systems, like the River Thames, are made use of for recreation and park linkage, *except where they are most needed.* The Victoria Embankment fails because it was never carried beyond its initial phase; and as a result, remains merely a reminder of what might have been. At Kingston, the very edge of the city's urban limits, the river commences to take on the func-

tions of a natural corridor with all the accompanying aesthetic and recreation uses imaginable—but this is out in the country!

London's green belt is more apparent on plan than in reality; and like Los Angeles, the city tends to sprawl without sense of direction or definition. The New Town Act of 1947 represents the most significant single act by the British government toward effectively controlling the city's future growth patterns. Now the north of London is blossoming through enforced economic development, burgeoning new towns and Los Angeles-style freeways, while the south remains fusty and congested. Only one new town, Crawley, has even been located south of London; and this is now considered to have been an economic blunder.

For sprawling, low-density cities, several medium-sized parks are usually preferrable to the single, large-park concept prevalent in the United States. But it remains necessary to prevent disassociation, by determining through systemization just what kind of relationships the various medium-sized parks will play in regard to their regional support, as well as in their relationship to each other. For instance, what facilities must be duplicated—as in the case of neighborhood parks? What facilities should remain unique? Perhaps the best solution for sprawling cities involves a three-tiered system which includes: the major or super parks (2,000 acres or more); medium-sized parks which duplicate facilities (100 acres or more); and as many neighborhood parks as needed (7-10 acres).

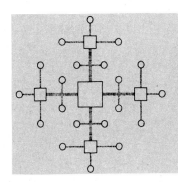

Diagrammatic relationship of three-tiered system having one central park, (New York Plan) four regional city parks, and twenty neighborhood or community parks.

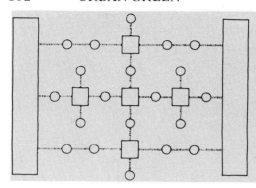

Diagrammatic relationship of three-tiered system having two peripheral super parks (Paris plan), five regional city parks, and eighteen neighborhood parks.

Paris—The Lungs and the Spine

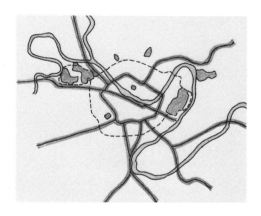

Since Paris is a densely compacted city, her need for parks and open space is great; but having a metropolitan area only one-third the size of London's, a different approach to systemization is possible.

Paris' two great lungs, the Bois de Boulogne and Vincennes, acting in conjunction with the Vie de Triomphe and the Seine, create the framework for a highly stylized urban system. Based on existing urbanography, a far-reaching plan by Haussmann and a penchant for both density and élan, Paris as one recalls emerged in the 19th Century as the most exciting and urban city of Europe. Her two super parks help to separate the city proper from her inner suburbs and are themselves connected across the heart of the city by the river and the Vie de Triomphe (Champs Elysees and accoutrements). In this fashion, Paris remains distinct from her immediate surroundings in a way which has rarely been accomplished elsewhere. Inner city green space is provided by such medium-sized parks as Luxembourg, Buttes-Chaumont, Jardin des Plantes, Montouris, and the Tuilleries.

Because Paris is relatively compact, a system of tree-lined boulevards and avenues, having ample space for the pedestrian, replaces the need for additional inner parks and, at the same time, helps to create linkage between existing parks, civic spaces, structures and monuments. In many ways, Paris *becomes* a park and does away with the need for a great number of escapist oases.

A new system of self-contained satellite cities, based on the London plan, was launched in 1961; but it will require still another decade before Paris can hope to catch up with existing physical shortages.

Copenhagen and Amsterdam—Concentric Green Rings and a Three-Fingered Hand

The physical histories of Copenhagen and Amsterdam are readily discernable from their city maps. They unfold before us like growth rings taken from a tree section, telling of their organic development over the centuries—the slow, methodical early years, structured Renaissance elegance, chaos of the 19th and 20th Centuries, and postwar organization.

Copenhagen's growth through the years is also read in her system of defenses. In the 14th and 18th Centuries, green rings consisting of fortified moats fanned out from the harbor to encircle the city. Though the defenses proved unsuccessful, they have given the city an instrument of urban continuity, as corridor parks.

Amsterdam's traditional canals, which radiate from the city's center like ripples in a pool, offer both a means of civic separation on the radial axis and continuity in concentric movement. Traveling radially toward the city's heart is like peeling an onion as one crosses this series of tree-lined canals, while a journey along the canals by boat provides a slower but, nevertheless, effective way of moving about the city.

Amsterdam's modern plan calls for linear development in three directions from the city's heart—like a three-fingered hand thumb, index and little finger. Replacing the ring and forefinger are narrow green spaces of agriculture and recreational development. This interlacing of rural and urban fingers gives structure to the city's growth patterns and maintains contact with nature as well. The super park, Amsterdamse Bos, represents one such green finger and offers 2500 acres of carefully planned watery wilderness to the nearby citizenry—easily within cycling distance. The middle finger, extending out from the city is represented by the new town of Amstelveen. A model city from every standpoint, it has been carefully planned to include a system of linking greenways and canals while, at the same time, having boundaries which are fixed permanently by adjacent parks and polders. Although it was invented by the American, Frederick Law Olmsted, the corridor park is probably seeing its greatest development in the cities of Northern Europe.

Stockholm—Tracery of Greenways

It is said that Swedes, like Englishmen, don't much like their cities; and when forced to endure them, bring along to them as much of the woods and the farm as possible. Both London and Stockholm are deliberately rich in public green space, although they differ considerably in approaches to park systemization.

Unlike London's great, disconnected parks, the public spaces of Stockholm are joined through an interlocking network of sinuous greenery which undulates through the city, squeezing under or leaping over traffic arterials, surrounding commercial centers, and flowing out to sea along the spiny ridges of the Baltic coast.

No one in Stockholm is ever really out of touch with this web of green. Residents of the city's many satellites may walk or cycle along its wooded pathways for miles without crossing streets. The new apartment complexes, both in Stockholm and her surrounding satellites, are planned in harmony with the city parks and connecting green corridors, which allow one to walk from apartment to shops without leaving the park's leafy embrace. At Fårsta and other new satellite communities, apartment dwellers push shopping carts to the market, take a stroll through the neighborhood or walk a quarter of a mile to the beach for a swim—without ever leaving the park!

Stockholm has achieved what Philadelphia's long range planners have evidently longed for, and may yet achieve—a park system, well-organized and large enough to exert a force upon urban expansion—to turn the tables on city growth in effect by separating identifiable urban complexes and, hence, to control their shape and growth by surrounding them with park. We have seen the generally unproductive effects of urban corridors in the form of Los Angeles' freeways. Nevertheless, the potential for successful urban organization is very real by the proper planning of such corridors so as to protect urban and community integrity and, at the same time, carry city transportation through ribbons of green.

There is nothing in Stockholm's experience which cannot be duplicated elsewhere given the measure of local conditioning. Rather, this city's efforts represent achievements which must be studied by all western cities in their present search for salvation. Stockholm, Amsterdam, London and other European cities are working to develop unique solutions to individual problems, which they hope will prove successful in the struggle for their health and well-being. Every city must, with whatever assistance is available, do likewise; and their measure of success may very well be determined by their attitudes towards public green space.

And the problems inherent in focusing attention on such green spaces, as a potential solution to existing urban ills, are tremendous. If, for example, the neighborhood park represents the best opportunity in our times for development of community identity, as a nucleus for neighborhood organization, then most people in America are not aware of it. Polls conducted by Harvard students from the School of Design suggest that young people are well aware of the catalytic qualities of the local park and school, while their elders favor the closest strip-commercial areas, if they have any ideas on the subject at all. The average European city has little trouble of this kind. Its citizens tend to be more aware of the local park and its meaning to the neighborhood; but in American cities as witnessed in Boston, the parks may literally have to go to the people to plead their case.

What is the proper ratio of people per park acre depending

upon variations in climate, topography and historic development? Can Houston's emphasis on private control remain valid in the face of imminent environmental chaos? Likewise, does Stockholm's rigid control of urban development permit sufficient latitude for personal, individual growth? A comparison of these two cities, as representatives of extremes in approach to urban planning in western society, might prove interesting. The pioneers, both fiercely independent and suspicious of their neighbors, have tended toward maladjustment when crowded and forced to conform, as pointed out in the frontier of 19th Century westward expansion. A pioneer ethic remains with us today, dictating the simplistic moral virtues of Horatio Alger and Ronald Reagan. But the competitive spirit, so admired in certain areas of American acculturation, possesses a dangerous and wrathful side effect when confronted by the complexities of today's urban density.

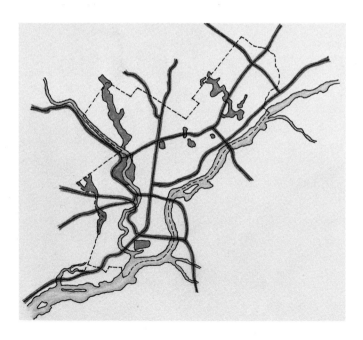

Philadelphia—Four Squares, Two Rivers, and a Great Green Wedge

The recent far reaching urban development in Philadelphia is in some ways a continuation of the original 1683 plan of William Penn, the city's founder. It is also a sign of hope to all American cities; in as much as, this city, more than any other, reflects the various stages of economic and political development through which the country has passed. Here is still seen the earliest plan, the green town envisioned by Penn, and still represented by the four large squares which ordered the plan's development. Here, as well, is Independence Mall connecting the two easterly squares by way of a great swath of green and, thereby, linking the central open space system with the nation's early history.

The destructive forces of the Machine Age are also evident in Philadelphia. As it passed from country town to industrial metropolis at a rate of expansion second only to New York, the city soon lost its colonial charm and sense of open space in the tangle of tenements, factories, rails and walls. But hopeful signs for the city's future are appearing in the recent ambitious redevelopment program. Like skilled surgeons, the city's planners and architects have regenerated atrophied parts, scrubbed away amorphous overlays to expose past order, cut away cancerous growth and gangrenous decay, and rejoined the city's future with its past. They labored mightily, but they had much to begin with—a solid historic foundation, so lacking in most American cities. The past and the future are comfortable together in Philadelphia. And so should they be, for such a relationship of style and purpose epitomizes the dynamics of orderly, organic development. Neither stagnant monotony in urban style or chaotic, bizarre lurches in architecture are healthy to a city's orderly progress—although we see both side by side in San Francisco, New York, and almost every large city in the United States.

Geographically the city is situated in the confluence of two rivers, the Delaware and the Schuylkill. It was, of course, the protected deep waters of the Delaware, just above the mouth of the smaller river, which made the original site a logical place for settlement. Historically the city faced the river; and again today, as a result of the redevelopment plans, the river orientation is being recognized. To the east lies the Schuylkill River watershed area, forming the backbone of the early city development. Here supporting the natural enclosing agents of wooded valley, river and ridgeline lies Fairmount Park, the largest developed city park in the world. Like a great green funnel, this 4,000-acre system of woods, streams and recreational areas angles into the city's heart, leaving the river at the urban core, in order to penetrate to the city's center.

Fairmount Park, acting as a physical boundary for the old city, connects the vast wooded tract of the Wissahickon Valley, the Schuylkill River Valley and the city's heart through the Benjamin Franklin Parkway, a broad tree-lined thoroughfare not unlike Paris' Champs Elysees. Moving in the opposite direction parallel to the Delaware River, another parkway system, connecting the parks along tree-lined Roosevelt Boulevard, joins the city to its physical northern boundary—the 1200 acre wooded park bordering Pennypack Creek. Urban expansion beyond Pennypack Park notwithstanding, the combination of these vast greenbelt parks, the connecting parkways, the rivers, stream valleys and central historic squares collaborate to give Philadelphia the best park system amongst American cities, (rivaled only by the Olmsted-Eliot system for Boston in late 19th Century). Hopefully the parks will keep pace with the city's overall renaissance. In Philadelphia, people are moving from the suburbs back to the center of the city. They will need an updating of the park system if this noble experiment is to be an unqualified success.

The American Indian, lacking a sense of virtuous competitiveness—even to the point of rejecting the concept of private property rights!—is today the object of pity and scorn. In Hawaii, both Eastern and Western immigrants possessed property drives which soon left the indigenous population dispossessed. This urge to succeed, and thereby defeat, has marked man's progress through history. Perhaps it also marks his destiny, in which case he may find it sooner than he anticipates, in an armageddon of chaos and despair.

Earth was mother to the Indian. He dared not sacrifice a hair of her head to profit; and she, in turn, protected and served him with all her abundance. In western culture, only the Scandinavians seem to understand the lessons of the indigenous American.

Territorial possession is a natural function of man and lower animals, writes Robert Ardrey, and therefore must remain an aspect of modern civilization. So be it. But territory to the individual may amount to farm, city or nation, whichever represents the greater force in his life as exemplified by the pioneer ethic, the classic Greek polis, or 18th Century European nationalism.

DeTocqueville, writing one-hundred years ago in *Democracy in America* noted:

> "The first thing that strikes observation is an unaccountable number of men, all equal and alike, incessantly endeavoring to produce the petty and paltry pleasures with which they glut their lives. Each of them living apart, is a stranger to the fate of all the rest—his children and his private friends constitute to him the whole of mankind; as for the rest of his fellow citizens, he is close to them but he feels them not; he exists but in himself and for himself alone; and if his kindred still remain to him, he may be said at any rate to have lost his country."

With perhaps superior vision, DeTocqueville was describing the "bubblemania" of today's American city and especially its suburbs. Perhaps someday the "territorial imperative" of Robert Ardrey will come to represent the earth collectively and its cities singly. Man's survival in the 21st Century may well depend upon it.

SYSTEMIZING THE URBAN GREEN: APPLICATIONS OF TECHNOLOGY AND SOCIOLOGY

"The park belongs to the people. Let's go take back the park!" So spoke the student body president in the Spring of 1969; and thousands of university students with an uncommon enthusiasm for city parks tore off into the streets of Berkeley to protect a tiny piece of real estate in that city, which young people had fashioned into a public park. Further south, the Recreation and Parks Commission of Los Angeles is treated to a demonstration by young rebels protesting a hastily-conceived ordinance which limits the size of park gatherings and the use of sound amplification equipment. Social action or reaction? In both instances, there were restrictions imposed by authority which produced the initial flare-ups. In Los Angeles, the good commissioners pursue the generation gap with a vengeance by refusing to grant permits to hold free performances by such groups as the "Hair" cast, even after the city council had previously given its blessing. The inequities and stress of urban America have long found outlets in the public park. Personal crime emerged in the immediate postwar period, racial unrest and injustices in the 50's and 60's and as for the 70's—adding to but not replacing the older problems—political, social, and even moral upheaval. Authority, predictably, has reacted in traditional fashion, to curb and control the excesses of our society. But a lot more is implied in their actions. Who, for instance, could have predicted such outraged reactions to basically straightforward limitations. (Reactions, at least in Berkeley, brought official counter-reaction, including shotgun death, heli-

copters, tear gas, mass incarceration without formal charges and three weeks of martial law.) Who, for that matter, could have predicted the need for such limitations in the first place—in a time when city parks are withering away? In view of ever-increasing, spectator-oriented commercialism as a satisfactory replacement for the troubled parks, the fact that mere green spaces can engender such demonstrations of loyalty and protection frightens and confuses many middle-aged Americans. Social action or reaction? Have the kids just discovered what DeTocqueville, Ardrey, Mumford and Jane Jacobs have been saying for so long and what, in turn, their elders have so long forgotten? What do these young people find in the park and, consequently, in themselves and each other which is so frightening to their elders? Hopefully, this book has already answered that question, at least in part. The important thing now is to bring a greater percentage of middle America back into the mainstream of youthful awareness. Back to a practicing urbanity. Back to a sense of public trust.

Social interaction and better use of park and town alike can and should be aided by the technology which has proved so destructive in the past. Now it must be put to work rebuilding.

For example, computer-aided method is available for purposes of data gathering, critical analysis, refinement of raw data and synthesis of materials into a developmental stage—ready for original programming and design interpretation. Computer graphics aid in the conceptualization of spatial organization by reproducing topography, geologic sections, plant communities, or any other existing or programmed phenomena, allowing park planners to produce design studies which have been pretested against natural and cultural criteria.

The sociological and ecological factors involved in modern urbanology are sufficiently complex as to become self-defeating without the aid of rapid and accurate data-processing techniques. Armed with computer-aided assistance and a method of procedure, a park planner can accurately measure a city's park needs and commence preparation of a program of park systemization. A procedural plan—towards the development of a park master plan—can be built on the following program:

1. First, understand the nature of the city, its physical character. This includes primarily its ecological base, its climate, geology, watershed, topography, soil and other salient natural conditions. It also includes existing man-made characteristics which add to the city's physical form and character. Ian McHarg, in *Design with Nature,* uses detailed analysis of a city's natural base to prove—or disprove—the logic of its man-made plan. Selecting Washington, D.C. for study, McHarg allows that even our least organically conceived or developed cities can, by careful consideration of natural phenomena, become healthy and successful—although a better location nearby for the location of the capital city was passed over. Pierre L'Enfant, in planning Washington, set the scheme, albeit fixed to his own time and country, for continued growth and development keyed to a somewhat self-conscious awareness of its status among cities and nations. Obviously the problems besetting the Capitol today have greatly damaged this image of democracy and humanism. Present conditions do not emanate from L'Enfant or Jefferson's 18th Century vision, however, but from 20th Century shortsightedness.

John Simonds, in *Landscape Architecture,* also deals with the natural base in urban design but more from an aesthetic rather than the ecologically-oriented position. Yet little has been accomplished in translating the natural sciences into the language of urban planners. The systemization of municipal parks depends upon such a translation being affected.

The nature of the city, especially its growth patterns, can be evaluated in economic terms as well. This involves not only population growth, increased buying power and a broader tax base, but changing patterns of leisure time. Characteristics of religious, social, and historic development are also considered to be part of the natural urban base.

2. Following a study of the city's natural base, a two-pronged investigation of park need should be undertaken.

    a. *Sociological Patterns*—A thorough analysis of neighborhood and residential character generally is made to determine behavioral trends and uncover areas of need within the program's jurisdiction. Results can be compared with existing facilities, space and programs to develop diagrams for ideal solutions.

    b. *Physical Patterns*—Starting from a basis of purely physical phenomena—natural and man-made—a study can be made to determine potential linkage systems, including sites for corridors and new parks. This is, of course, the exact opposite of the typical method of site selection in American cities—based largely on availability rather than suitability of land. The more logical attempt to establish a natural system of organic spatial relationship is, once again, found in Stockholm.

3. After completing the two-pronged analysis to determine both sociological and physical patterns of urban development, the final step calls for synthesis—a marriage of systems with differing criteria. Hopefully the juxtaposition of social, historic and economic factors over topographic, ecological and structural criteria will fit reasonably well; but in most cases, the differing bases of criteria defy synthesis. At this stage, park department and city officials generally may find themselves face to face with some difficult prospects. Compromises may be necessary. The synthesis of a people-oriented study will require it; but the city will have, at the very least, the beginnings of a plan.

4. The final stage in the development of a city-wide public park system is total synthesis—the transformation of concept into finite plan.

The kind of personnel needed to carry out the several stages of city park systemization—research, analysis, synthesis, conceptualization and master park plan—are available in every American city: Boy Scouts, college students, ecologists, artists, fund-raisers. All kinds of needed skills can be found and put to use by the enterprising park department. Those with organizing talents and good-idea people are important as well in helping to bring about a renaissance of city park activity. Under Thomas Hoving, the New York City park system initiated a number of recreational and social programs a few years ago. Evening concerts and dances were well attended. Sunday promenades and other special weekend activities were conducted as well. Hoving's departure for greener pastures ended the experiments, but the concept of planned activities *for all age levels* is just as sensible today. Rock concerts and dances will bring young people to the parks in droves. During the summer months, the Tuilleries Gardens in Paris are packed every night for chamber music concerts. Slides of the park's history are also shown and a few Roman candles burned in the Grande Bassin.

For this light, pleasant bit of entertainment, Parisians and tourists pay a dollar a head! Any summer evening in Philadelphia crowds will gather in John F. Kennedy Plaza to participate in free dance concerts under the stars. The park should be a proper place at night—not a hideout for lurking evil.

As always, programs in the park should emphasize active involvement rather than spectator entertainment. The Renaissance Pleasure Faire, held each May near Los Angeles, is successful by the extent to which entertainment is self-engendered. Here people have shown that they will gladly pay in order to dress themselves in 16th Century costumes and engage in such activities as "jousting" and "wenching."

Neighborhood carnivals, animal shows, insect zoos, amateur theatre, art shows, light shows, happenings, love-ins, you-name-it can all become a part of the local park's activities. Only the imagination limits the organizer's palette. (Nonverbal theatre, for example, was for this writer a recent and unexpected park treat.)

Idea people and civic organizers will find their local park administration more than anxious to cooperate—even when they consider the program hairbrained. (Experience dictates two precautions here: Advertise wherever possible, and avoid politics.)

Philadelphia has made the effort to bring people back to the city, and Boston has tried to bring the parks to the people. Even amidst civic chaos and dessication of the parks, it can be demonstrated that grass roots programs, like Boston's, can succeed. Imagination and determination may be all that is needed.

There are other ways in which the average citizen can help to support a viable, healthy park system. For one thing, support of open space legislation is essential. Land acquisition for park and recreation use must be greatly increased through new legislation as well as through federal grants. Massive new funding programs through federal taxes are needed immediately. Sixty percent of the federal taxes—some 300 million dollars per day—is consumed annually in national defense. This imbalance of expenditures is at least very shortsighted in view of the continually worsening domestic problems in the United States. More federal funds for local use, and legislation to expedite acquisition of parksites are needed now! Legislators advocating such measures should be supported loud and strong. The old pioneer ethic of America is not going to die with change. Rugged individualism is going to be as necessary tomorrow as it was yesterday; but tomorrow's urban densities will not permit aloofness or disregard for one's neighbor or his rights. He drinks from the same water supply. His lights also go out in a major power failure. He must breathe the same air. When all of the local area—for as many miles as one can drive—is filled with stores and houses, where there are no common places to walk other than streets and sidewalks, what then has private property and individual freedom left to offer the cities?

Individualism and American enterprise, those native traits we prize, can be just as effective in facing social needs as they always have been in solving technical problems. Facing them is the only problem.

Communal Interdependence—The City As Life

With the possible exception of hermits, beachcombers and uranium prospectors, people need cities. Conservationists, ecologists, oceanographers, Iowa farmers, explorers and even Londoners need cities—if only for economic reasons. Most of us need them for much more than the mere living they provide. We are, after all, a gregarious breed. According to the naturalists, we are more baboon than tiger—difficult as it may be to accept. It is unnatural for man to live the solitary life of the tiger or eagle. Much as he may attempt to emulate those noble creatures, man is simply not prepared, emotionally or physically, to achieve his ends through a single family unit. What a lucky break. Man's interdependence, whether or not a psychic weakness, has enabled the human species, through cooperative effort, to achieve high levels of specialization and density. The prospector and hermit, like the tiger, have to do everything for themselves. They must produce their food as well as their clothing and shelter—even entertainment (which isn't so bad an idea provided virtuosity is not demanded). The solitary family unit is able to disperse its basic chores and, therefore, manage to live in reasonable comfort; but the internal dependencies of rural life deprive each member of growth in spirit and wisdom due to a lack of peer group associations.

By living together as a community, we humans have learned to divide the tasks thus allowing for the development of skills and, in doing so, shortened the time necessary for accomplishment. The same work gets done in less time by encouraging specialization. It also comes out better. The rugged individualist—like the tiger—may take pride in being able to do everything; but as a result of this necessity, he is never able to concentrate and thoroughly develop his best talents. And a society of such people can never become a culture, because there are no interdependencies established. It is a rural community, having its living units as far apart as possible, with no restrictions against dumping garbage or storing junked cars on the front stoop.

The city, on the other hand, is the result of communal inter-dependency, in which the development of skill and talent becomes a natural result of community life. The major products of specialization and diversity found in the city are:

1. Development of skill (technology),
2. Increase of efficiency (leisure), and
3. Development of creativity (art).

A community which excells in any or all of these has an economic advantage (trade) over its neighbors, and may grow rich and powerful, as did the Dutch cities of the 14th Century.

People need cities in order to grow as individuals, to develop their individual talents as well as to benefit from the skills and talents of others. Our individual lives are richer for having as neighbors the carpenter as well as the violinist. Raising children is easier and less frightening because others are doing the same, just as being a plumber, teacher or bank president is not so dull because others nearby are doing something else.

The city is far more meaningful to each man than merely the providing of a livelihood. Despite a century of dehumanizing technological achievement, the potential for enrichment and stimulation remains. People need each other; therefore, they need cities. And cities need parks.

Aside from their obvious physical attributes—the things which impress the professionals, like greenbelts, spatial relief, balance and open space—cities need parks; because they represent urban man's highest achievement in communal interdependence. The parks depend upon a sense of public trust for their very existence; and in return, they provide a base, as in ancient Athens, for public exchange through technology, leisure and art. City people, therefore, need parks. The sylogism is complete.

*Rome.   Brought by aqueduct from classic times, the
neighborhood water supply is seen as a catalyst for local
interaction—a forerunner of the neighborhood park
system.*

Valingby, Sweden. A carefully planned attempt to introduce open green space as separator between commercial and residential development—a balancing void between architectural masses. Below: An unneeded street separates a neighborhood park from a space-starved elementary school in a California town—a victim of gridiron planning.

Los Angeles. Lemon Grove mini-park. The tot-lot, vest pocket park, or recreation center as a partial solution is providing for recreation needs in older neighborhoods or where severe space limitations exist.

Stockholm.   Midsummer festival at the edge of Malaren Sea. Urban space and the public trust—bulwarks against incapsulation (Courtesy Text and Bilder).

Pedestrian underpass to MacArthur Park, Los Angeles (Courtesy Harvey Steinberg).

Stockholm. Ralambshoosparken. Separation of vehicular and pedestrian ways—first used effectively in city park design by F.L. Olmsted in the 1851 design of Central Park (New York). Here it is employed in Stockholm, allowing the continuation of the park (Courtesy Gosta Glase).

The same purpose is served in development of a suburban center, near Stockholm (Courtesy Gosta Glase).

Stockholm. Ralambsparken.   Not as disconnected enties, but as continuously flowing space, the city's parks weave a web of green through the urban structure, under roadways (above) and along the water corridors (right) (Courtesy Leif Perrson, Gosta Glase).

Stockholm. Gardetpark. Only the "super parks" (2,000 acres or more) are large enough to bring to bear upon the adjacent urban structure the force to form that structure—give it scale and balance. Their great size provides a breadth of uses in different seasons. The tower is the tallest building in Sweden! (Courtesy Peter Blom).

Het Amsterdamse Bos. (Courtesy Dienst Publieke Werken.)

Chicago. Jackson Park (Courtesy Chicago Park District).

Amsterdam. Het Amsterdamse Bos. The "super park" in winter (Courtesy Dienst Publieke Werken).

Amsterdam. Het Amsterdamse Bos.   With the land literally salvaged from the sea, a magnificent new super park as controlling instrument against urban sprawl (Courtesy Dienst Publieke Werken).

Los Angeles. Hansen Park. Restricted, low density usage imposed by golf.

Los Angeles. Griffith Park.   The rugged, forested terrain of the city's greatest park undergoing a "soften-ing" operation necessary for the installation of the new Roosevelt Golf Course. Golf makes money for the city and is therefore popular with the park board (Courtesy Los Angeles City Recreation and Park Department).

Los Angeles. Malibu Cañon.   *The Renaissance Pleasure Faire. The pleasure comes from dressing up and entertaining each other—a hopeful sign.*

Los Angeles. Malibu Cañon.

EPILOGUE

To a child, the best parts of a park are the parts that are the least maintained. It is his nature to be attracted to the slopes, the bushes, the long grass, the waterside. . . . But what do authorities do? They exploit our wealth to make improvements for the worse. They invade the parks, erecting kiosks and tea gardens, and side shows for those who require their entertainment ready made. . . . The trend is universal. . . . Having cleared away the places, deposit junk in them, and create "Adventure Playgrounds" so called, the equivalent of creating Whipsnades for wildlife instead of erecting actual cages!*

Writing in *Children's Games in Street and Playground,* Peter and Iona Opie are obviously reflecting the values of children, not park officials. Adults, and especially the official sort, tend to approach park and recreation programming by reacting to potential hazards rather than acting upon obvious need.

Sometimes this reaction to hazards or "undesirable" aspects of public park life reaches the ultimate level of negative thinking, resulting in the aborting of a park program or even a park. In the summer of 1969, for example, local distaste for alleged homosexual gatherings resulted in the physical destruction of a Bronx, New York neighborhood park. It's gone forever. No fear of deviates plagues the community now. No grass, no trees, no noisy kids at play. Only resting automobiles. Closing or destroying the park to keep out the blacks, the browns, and socially undesirable is not a new theme for the seventies. It's as old as ignorance and fear. Fear of strangers in our parks is sometimes equaled by fear of youth. At People's Park in Berkeley, Griffith Park in Los Angeles, and countless young people's gathering throughout the country—in and out of city parks—nervous elders have banded together to limit young people's organized activities. Court injunctions and administrative impedance have cancelled the Renaissance Pleasure Faire, the free "Hair" concert in Griffith Park, and countless rock festivals across the breadth of the country. The aged park habitues are likewise seen as undesirables, as evidenced by their planned segregation into "senior citizens" areas and the elimination of benches in downtown malls. Like the young people who were driven off of Sunset Boulevard in Los Angeles a few years ago, the elderly have little money to spend and are, therefore, somewhat of a nuisance to the business community.

Middle America, in its drive to create a sense of civic spirit and cultural awareness, thinks in terms of Lincoln Center and the Atlanta Civic Auditorium. But culture is more of a grass-roots phenomenon. In the case of young people, it must be nurtured through their truly good music and art, and especially through their own social infrastructures, which is very real if often misunderstood by their elders. Artificial culture, that which is borrowed from other places, other times, may fail to capture the admiration of all but a few of the super educated (and super snobs). Atlanta's disasterous experiment in "cultural revival" provides a lesson for all civic-minded people. The now bankrupt civic auditorium associ-

*Children's Games in Street and Playground, Oxford, 1970.

127

ation may simply have misread the city's definitions of culture. During a high school disturbance in Los Angeles recently in (of all places) a music class, a black student was quoted as saying, "Who cares about Bach? We don't want that old dead music. Give us the Supremes." Young people everywhere—yes, even in Europe—would understand his sentiment; but for Middle America, it was just another example of cultural poverty. (A brief, personal questionnaire, at the time, demonstrated an almost unbelievable generation gap in that virtually no one over 40 saw any value in the black student's point of view.) Cultivating the tastes of black students in Los Angeles to the levels of chamber music in the Tuilleries Gardens is not the question. Better to probe for the best within the existing cultural melieu.

And just as park play equipment is selected by adults—for its aesthetic appeal, pesticides are depended upon to preserve the carpetlike purity of park lawns, despite their tendency to exterminate the birds and squirrels. In Milan a special arm of the city police skulk in the parks in hopes of catching youthful soccer players on the precious turf. Called *verdoni*, or grass cops, they demonstrate the city's loyalty to appearance over kids. The generation gap is not limited to American shores and, as always, becomes intensified in city parks, whatever the cause. But parks are for people, including those whose life styles differ from the "norm." Parks are for kids, with all their accompanying noise and irritations. Age in either direction should not be a factor in park segregation or denial. (Old people don't really scare kids anyway—only their mothers.)

But the park concept remains free of commercialism and fear. Neither the time spent in parks or the real estate can be measured in monetary values. Nor can the park function as intended in a climate of mistrust or disassociation. Bubblemania, the psychosis of urban incapsulation, breeds on the break-up of social institutions—and can prove to be fatal, especially to the park.

Those who doubt this should visit any of the more "backward" towns and cities of Europe, South America, the Orient, or even parts of United States where incapsulation has not yet become a decisive factor in urban development. Here one can still observe public park functions long forgotten in Houston and Detroit. In Guadalajara and Stockholm, public promenades occupy the parks on summer evenings. The sidewalk cafes of Paris and the piazzas of Rome are still crowded with lounging citizens—relaxing, talking, watching the girls, enjoying the company of people. Every fall, summer and spring evening the tree-shaded little green squares of Athens are crowded with people demonstrating the vitality and meaning of urbanity through the simple pleasures of camaraderie and neighborliness.

Some of this spirit of urbanity remains in United States—in downtown ghettoes, a few "backward" communities of the nation, and amongst young people almost everywhere. Those who have gathered at weekend rock festivals or any of the more permanent youthful communes have clearly expressed their desire to escape from the materialistic, encapsulated world of their elders, cut off by television, automobiles, single family boxes, stratified housing tracts and single purpose lives.

The factors of urban life, which made the city park a necessity to life in the city, are just as real today as they were in the grimy coke-towns of industrial England a hundred years ago. In many ways, things are worse today, and the escape route to the suburbs has not proven wholly satisfactory even to the few who have escaped. Like the pioneers and homesteaders of a century past, we have continued to seek greener pastures—to move on when the old farm was worn out. The pioneer ethic robs us of our sense of public welfare, and makes us a nation of wastemakers. We can, however, overcome the waste ethic and make our cities livable again if we want to. It's that simple, but we must decide on a basic reassessment of our values. Private property or public trust? Mechanical time or flow of life? The city parks can provide so much in a reconstructed urban society; or they can be left to die, together with public trust and urban culture in general. The time for action is upon us.

BIBLIOGRAPHY

Part I

Bacon, Edmund, *Design of Cities*, New York, 1967.

Chadwick, George, *The Park and the Town*, London, 1966.

Church, Richard, *The Royal Parks of London*, London, 1956.

Clifford, Derek, *A History of Garden Design*, London, 1959.

Downing, Andrew, *Landscape Gardening*, New York and London, 1844.

Fabos, Julius, *Frederick Law Olmsted*, Jr., New York, 1968.

Fariello, Francesco, *Architectura dei Giardini*, Rome, 1967.

Geddes, Patrick, *Cities in Evolution*, London, 1915.

Goodman, Paul and Percival, *Communitas*, New York, 1947.

Howard, Ebeneezer, *Garden Cities of Tomorrow*, London, 1898.

Hubbard, V. and Kimball, T., *An Introduction to the Study of Landscape Architecture*, New York, 1924.

Masson, Georgina, *Italian Gardens*, New York, 1966.

Mumford, Lewis, *The City in History*, New York, 1961.

New York Park Department, City of, *Twenty-eight Years of Progress*, New York, 1962.

Olmsted, Frederick Law, *Walks and Talks of An American Farmer in England*, London, 1852.

Robinson, William, *The Parks, Gardens and Promenades of Paris*, London, 1869.

Zucker, Paul, *Town and Square*, New York and London, 1959.

Part II

Ardrey, Robert, *African Genesis*, New York, 1963.

Ardrey, Robert, *The Territorial Imperative*, New York, 1966.

Cullen. Gordon, *Townscape*, London, 1961.

Eckbo, Garrett, *Landscape for Living*, New York, 1949.

Editors of Fortune, *The Exploding Metropolis*, New York, 1958.

Hall, Edward, *The Hidden Dimension*, New York, 1969.

Jacobs, Jane, *The Death and Life of Great American Cities*, New York, 1962.

Keats, John, *Crack in the Picture Window*, 1956.

Lynch, Kevin, *The Image of the City*, Boston, 1958.

Mumford, Lewis, *The Urban Prospect*, New York, 1968.

Neutra, Richard, *Survival Through Design*, New York, 1954.

Park Department Annual Reports and Data Sheets:

Chicago	Philadelphia
St. Louis	Stuttgart
Stockholm	Denver
Amsterdam	Boston
Copenhagen	Salt Lake City
San Francisco	Cleveland
New York	Pittsburgh

Phoenix Gallery, *People's Park*, New York, 1970.

Simonds, John O., *Landscape Architecture* (revised), 1970.

Part III

Carr, Donald, *Breath of Life*, New York, 1965.

Ehrlich, Paul, *The Population Bomb*, New York, 1968.

Fromm, Erich, *May Man Prevail*, New York, 1961.

Josephson, Eric and Mary (ed.), *Man Alone*, New York, 1962.

McHarg, Ian, *Design with Nature*, New York, 1968.

Opie, Peter and Iona, *Children's Games in Streets and Playgrounds*, London, 1970.

President's Council on Recreation and Natural Beauty, *From Sea to Shining Sea*, Washington, D.C., 1968.

Report of Fairmont Park Association, 1969.